BY THE EDITORS OF

CONSUMER GUIDE®

FAT
COUNTER

GUIDE

D0840955

☐ ☐ ☐ ☐ ☐

PUBLICATIONS INTERNATIONAL, LTD.

Louis Weber, C.E.O
Publications International, Ltd.
7373 N. Cicero Avenue
Lincolnwood, Illinois 60646

ISBN: 0-7853-1565-9

Notice:
Neither the Editors of Consumer Guide® and
Publications International, Ltd., nor the
publisher take responsibility for any possible
consequences from the use of material in this
publication. The publisher advises the reader to
check with a physician before beginning any
dietary program or therapy. This publication
does not take the place of your physician's
recommendations for diet modification. Every
effort has been made to assure that the
information in this publication is accurate and
current at the time of printing.

Contents

Introduction

WHY WORRY ABOUT FAT?

Your diet affects a lot more than just your waistline. Food choices and eating habits influence not only the shape of your body but your overall health as well.

Fat is a big part of the American diet. Fully 37 percent of the total calories we consume come from fat, most of which is saturated fat. Compared with many countries around the world, our consumption of saturated fat and cholesterol is unusually high.

Although we need some fat in our diet for good health, too much of it can have exactly the opposite effect. Clearly, dietary fat can make foods so appealing that they're hard to resist. That's why we have to be especially careful in choosing foods.

This introduction will start with a consideration of the immediate danger that a diet high in saturated fat and cholesterol poses to your heart. Then we'll look at some of the other health risks associated with a high-fat diet, including its links to cancer and obesity. Next we'll try to give you a more complete understanding of what fat and cholesterol are and what roles they play in the body. Finally, we will explain some simple dietary guidelines to follow for planning and enjoying a healthier low-fat diet.

One of the main reasons to adopt a low-fat diet is to combat coronary heart disease (CHD)—the formation of fatty deposits and blood clots on the walls of the coronary arteries, which supply blood to the heart muscle. Over time, a buildup of these deposits leads to a narrowing of the arteries. This causes a reduction in the flow of blood to the heart, just as stepping on a garden hose cuts down the flow of water to a lawn sprinkler.

Coronary heart disease is often called a silent killer because the deposits that clog the arteries build up gradually over the course of many years, often without giving any warning of what may lie ahead. Sometimes, the first symptom of CHD is a pain or an uncomfortable tightness, squeezing, or pressure of the chest, referred to as angina.

Although the heart is usually thought of in more dramatic terms, basically it is a muscle—an extraordinarily important and durable muscle, to be sure, but like all muscles, one that requires nourishment to survive. And that nourishment is carried in the blood.

A heart attack occurs when the blood flow through a coronary artery to a portion of the heart is completely blocked and part of the heart muscle dies. If enough of the heart muscle is damaged, the victim may die. Unfortunately, for a large number of people, the first indication of CHD is the crushing pain from a serious and potentially fatal heart attack. The statistics tell the story: Heart attacks strike 1.25 million Americans each year, killing more than half a million of them. CHD is the leading cause of death in the United States.

INTRODUCTION

Though it strikes many older people, CHD is not limited to the elderly. Indeed, nearly half of all heart attacks occur in people under the age of 65. What's more, the fatty deposits that may eventually block the arteries of adults can begin to form in childhood. CHD is not necessarily a part of growing older, however. You can take steps *now* to protect your own heart and to reduce the possibility of one day becoming a heart attack statistic.

While some of the factors that increase your risk of CHD are beyond your control—such as being male or having a family history of heart disease—there are three major risk factors that you *can* control: cigarette smoking, high blood pressure, and a high level of cholesterol in the blood. If you smoke, you *can* stop. If you have high blood pressure, you *can* work with your doctor to get it under control. And if you have a high blood cholesterol level, you *can* make dietary changes to help reduce it. **Decreasing the amount of saturated fat in your diet is the most important way to reduce blood cholesterol levels.** And that's one area where this *Fat Counter Guide* can help: It provides not only the values for fat and saturated fat, but it also gives percentages of calories from those two sources for most foods—a more useful and, in many ways, more accurate way to measure your dietary fat and saturated fat intake.

The benefits of a diet low in fat go well beyond reducing the risks of heart disease. The most common cancers found in this country, cancer of the breast, prostate, and colon, are also linked to high-fat diets.

For example, studies of various population groups show that people who eat a lot of fresh fruits and vegetables and consume whole-grain breads and cereals may receive protection from colon cancer because of the dietary fiber and vitamins these foods contain. But here again, fat in the diet has an impact. Perhaps most importantly, it affects bile, which the body produces to digest and absorb fat. The more fat there is in the diet, the more bile there will be available for delivery to the colon. Though some bile is necessary, too much of it may damage colon cells, possibly leading to tumors. There are, of course, many other factors, but the fat connection should not be overlooked.

It would be misleading to oversimplify a complex issue and imply that a low-fat diet will protect against these cancers. These are complicated diseases; much is unknown about them. The fundamental point is that a low-fat diet is clearly helpful in combating CHD, and it may have a beneficial influence with regard to cancer protection.

WHAT IS FAT?

Fat is nature's storehouse of energy-yielding fuel. Most fats are made up primarily of **triglycerides**— three fatty-acid chains attached to a glycerol molecule. To use the energy stored in fat, the body breaks down triglycerides into fatty acids. Individual cells then oxidize, or burn, the fatty acids for energy. Protein and carbohydrates such as sugars and starches also provide energy, but fat, with over two times the energy available per gram, is a denser fuel.

INTRODUCTION

All living things, including plants, have the ability to manufacture fatty acids and assemble them into molecules of fat to store energy. Different species tend to manufacture different types of fat. As a general rule, animals manufacture a fat composed mainly of **saturated** fatty acids, and plants manufacture a fat that is rich in **polyunsaturated** fatty acids. Some plants also manufacture fat that contains a good deal of **monounsaturated** fatty acids, which are similar to polyunsaturated fatty acids but are much less complex. (The terms *saturated* and *unsaturated* refer to the number of hydrogen atoms found in the fatty acids that make up dietary fat: Saturated fats have the maximum number of hydrogen atoms; polyunsaturated fats have the fewest.) The degree of saturation determines which form (solid or liquid) the fat takes at room temperature, how useful it is for various cooking and baking needs, and how it affects your blood cholesterol levels.

Fats that consist primarily of saturated fatty acids are called **saturated fats**. They are typically solid at room temperature. Butter, lard, and the marbling and visible fat in meats are saturated fats. Much of the fat in milk (butterfat) is also saturated and solid at room temperature, but the process of homogenization breaks the fat into fine particles and scatters it throughout the liquid portion of the milk.

Polyunsaturated fats, on the other hand, are usually liquid at room temperature. These liquid oils are found mostly in the seeds of plants. The oils from safflowers, sunflowers, corn, soybeans, and cotton are polyunsaturated fats made up primarily of polyunsaturated fatty acids.

Like polyunsaturated fats, **monounsaturated fats** are also liquid at room temperature. Examples of fats rich in monounsaturated fatty acids are olive oil and canola (or rapeseed) oil. Avocados and nuts are also rich in this fat.

Sometimes vegetable oils are chemically modified to change some of their polyunsaturated fatty acids to saturated ones. This process, called **hydrogenation**, is useful commercially because it improves the shelf life of the oils and allows the less expensive vegetable oils to acquire important baking properties that are normally found in the more costly animal fats. **Hydrogenated** or **partially hydrogenated** vegetable oils are more saturated than the original oils from which they're made. Margarine and vegetable shortening are examples of such vegetable oils.

Although most animal fats are saturated and most vegetable fats unsaturated, there are some noteworthy exceptions. Fish and chicken fats have fewer saturated fatty acids and more polyunsaturated fatty acids than do red meats such as beef, veal, lamb, and pork. The fat from fish is actually so rich in polyunsaturated fatty acids that at room temperature it takes the form of an oil, just like fats usually found only in vegetables.

By the same token, a few vegetable fats are so rich in saturated fats that they are solid at room temperature. Palm oil, coconut oil, and palm kernel oil contain between 50 and 80 percent saturated fat. Coconut oil and palm oil are widely used

in the commercial production of nondairy cream-
ers, snacks such as popcorn or chips, baked goods,
and candy bars. Cocoa butter, the fat found in expensive chocolates, is also rich in saturated fatty
acids.

Foods rich in fat are usually those prepared by
frying, basting, or marinating in butter, margarine,
oil, or drippings from meats and poultry. Fat-rich
foods can also be detected by their greasy textures.
Sometimes fat can be seen as a solid whitish substance found around the perimeter of a cut of meat
or running through it. In poultry, most of the fat
comes from the skin. Dairy products such as whole
milk, ice cream, whipped cream, and most cheeses
are also rich sources of saturated fat. Sometimes,
however, it's hard to spot the fat in foods. For example, commercially prepared baked goods like
pies, cakes, and cookies are common sources of
hidden fats. Although we may think of them only
as "sweets," they are often prepared with hydrogenated oils that provide hefty doses of saturated
fatty acids.

THE IMPORTANCE OF FAT

Humans also have the ability to manufacture fat.
When you provide your body with more energy
than it can use right away, it packages that energy
into fat and stores it. The energy that your body
uses comes from fuels in the foods you eat. (Carbohydrate and fat are the primary energy-yielding
fuels, but under some limited circumstances protein can also be used for energy. Alcohol can be another fuel available to the body.)

The amount of energy that can be obtained from a particular food is represented by the number of **calories** it produces when it is burned in the body. When you consume excess energy from food, that extra energy is stored in the body as fat. Recent research suggests that if the extra energy is provided by carbohydrate, the body may step up its metabolism and heat is produced. This is more likely to be the case if the person is physically active. In other words, if you exercise you can eat almost all the calories you want without being worried about excess body fat—as long as the calories come from carbohydrate. It is only when excess energy is consumed from fat and not from either carbohydrate or protein that this excess energy is likely to be stored as fat. (Alcohol is an exception to this general rule, since sometimes energy consumed from alcohol can be stored as body fat.)

We all need some stored fat to provide our bodies with energy at times when we're not eating. Body fat is especially important as a source of energy during the night, because vital functions such as breathing and circulation require energy even while you're asleep. During pregnancy and childbirth, women acquire additional fat to support the fetus and to provide energy for the strain of labor and the production of milk after delivery.

Besides serving as stored energy, body fat has several practical purposes. A cushion of fat distributed at strategic places throughout the body protects the heart, lungs, kidneys, and other organs from injury. And a layer of fat found just below the skin helps insulate us from heat loss.

INTRODUCTION

Women have more body fat than men. A certain amount of fat in women is necessary to initiate and maintain menstruation. The increase in body fat appears in adolescence and is a natural physical consequence of maturation.

The amount of fat in your body varies, depending on how much energy your body has stored. Only when an adult continually consumes more calories than the body needs for vital functions, daily activities, and exercise does body fat begin to accumulate, causing weight gain. Besides detracting from physical appearance and causing psychological distress, excessive body fat is also harmful to your health. Diabetes, high blood pressure, and heart disease are but a few of the health risks of being overweight.

FAT IN THE BLOOD

Like cholesterol, some fat is normally found in the blood; it travels through the bloodstream from the food source or body stores to the cells that use it. Fat needs lipoproteins to carry it through the bloodstream. To illustrate how important these lipoproteins are for fat transport, drop a tablespoon of oil or a pat of butter into a glass of water and watch what happens. The fat and water repel each other. This reaction makes the transportation of fat through blood difficult. When fat is encased in a lipoprotein that prevents it from mixing with blood, however, it can move effortlessly through the bloodstream.

Although all lipoproteins carry some triglycerides (fat molecules), the chylomicrons and the very-low-density lipoproteins (VLDLs) are the primary movers of triglyceride. Each transports triglycerides from a particular source.

When dietary fat is digested in the body, the fatty acids are released and then packaged into triglycerides in the intestines. The chylomicrons pick up these triglycerides, along with dietary cholesterol, and transport them through the blood to the muscle cells and fat cells. An enzyme residing on these cells breaks down the chylomicrons so that the fatty acids can enter the cells. The dietary cholesterol is left behind in the remnant, which makes its way to the liver. The enzyme works quickly: Within five minutes, it can clear from the blood half the triglycerides absorbed from a meal. Within a few hours after a meal, the enzyme will have removed all the chylomicrons from the blood.

When your body makes its own fat in order to store extra calories from food, a different lipoprotein takes care of transportation. The VLDLs carry the fat that is made in the liver, along with cholesterol, to the cells where the fat is stored. Once the VLDLs have dropped off their triglycerides, they contain mostly cholesterol and evolve into low-density lipoprotein (LDL) molecules.

WHAT IS CHOLESTEROL?
Cholesterol is a white, odorless, fatlike substance that is a basic component of the human body. In fact, each cell in the body is protected by a covering made up partly of cholesterol. It is an essential part of the chemistry of human beings. Cholesterol is also used to make bile, a greenish fluid produced

by the liver and stored in the gallbladder. The body needs bile to digest foods that contain fat and to absorb cholesterol from food. In addition, bile is needed to absorb vitamins A, D, E, and K (the fat-soluble vitamins). Indeed, cholesterol is so vital to our health that our bodies can make all the cholesterol we need. Whether we need it or not, however, we also get it from many of the foods we eat, though you can't taste it or see it on your plate. All animals produce cholesterol, and all foods that come from animal sources, such as meat, eggs, milk, cheese, and butter, contain cholesterol. Plants, on the other hand, do not manufacture cholesterol. All plant foods, such as cereals, grains, nuts, fruits, vegetables, and vegetable oils, contain no cholesterol.

CHOLESTEROL IN THE BLOOD

Some cholesterol is always present in the blood because the blood helps to transport cholesterol through the body. But cholesterol is one of a group of substances known as lipids (fats), which do not dissolve or mix with water. Blood happens to be made up of a substantial amount of water. Consequently, in order to move cholesterol through the bloodstream, the body wraps it in protein to form a molecule called a lipoprotein. Thus the lipoproteins glide through the bloodstream like microscopic submarines, carrying their cargo of cholesterol through the body.

If cholesterol is normally present in your blood, why should you worry about it? The reason is that the total amount of blood cholesterol reveals how efficiently your body is using and managing its cholesterol. Excess cholesterol in the blood may mean that something is going wrong with the body's balancing mechanism.

Two types of lipoproteins play a major role in moving cholesterol through the blood. Low-density lipoproteins, or LDLs, carry cholesterol to the body's cells, where it can be used in a variety of ways. In contrast, high-density lipoproteins, or HDLs, are thought to carry cholesterol from the cells back to the liver so it can be absorbed in the bile and removed from the body.

When more of the cholesterol in your blood is being carried by HDLs, there is less danger of an accumulation of cholesterol in the body. For that reason, HDLs are often referred to as "good" cholesterol. If, on the other hand, most of the cholesterol in your blood is being carried by LDLs, there is an increased danger that cholesterol may accumulate in the body. This is where the problem for your heart lies. The LDLs, which are often referred to as "bad" cholesterol, may take some of the unused cholesterol and deposit it on the walls of your coronary arteries. Over time, this buildup can begin to block the flow of blood to the heart, leading to a heart attack.

Periodic testing to measure the amount of cholesterol in the blood is important because such tests reveal how efficiently your body handles cholesterol. The most common test measures total cholesterol. Another test, lipoprotein analysis, determines how much of that cholesterol is in the form of HDLs and how much in LDLs.

WHAT CAUSES HIGH BLOOD CHOLESTEROL?

The body has several mechanisms that enable it to balance the cholesterol it produces against what it obtains from food. When your diet provides a substantial amount of cholesterol, the body's output of cholesterol may be reduced. The body can also shed some excess cholesterol by using it to make bile and by dissolving some cholesterol in the bile that leaves the body through the feces.

These mechanisms aren't foolproof, however. In a very small minority of people (perhaps less than one percent of all those who have high blood cholesterol), an inherited defect can cause blood cholesterol levels to rise. This defect interferes with special receptor cells, located mainly on the surface of the liver, which are responsible for pulling cholesterol out of LDL molecules. When these receptors don't function properly, LDL cholesterol is stranded in the bloodstream.

For the vast majority of people whose blood cholesterol levels are too high, the major factor is not heredity. The problem is caused by diets that are high in total fat, saturated fat, and cholesterol.

HOW DIETARY FAT AFFECTS BLOOD CHOLESTEROL

The relationship between dietary fat and blood cholesterol is a close one. However, not all sources of fat have the same impact on cholesterol. Saturated fat disturbs the body's cholesterol balance more than unsaturated fat does. For reasons that are not well understood, saturated fats suppress the production of LDL receptors, the ones responsible for pulling cholesterol out of the bloodstream. As a result, the total amount of cholesterol in the blood rises. Thus, **saturated fats in the diet tend to increase blood cholesterol.** In fact, no other dietary factor increases blood cholesterol as much as a high intake of saturated fat.

On the other hand, **polyunsaturated fats tend to lower total cholesterol levels** *when they replace saturated fats in the diet.* This is an important distinction to keep in mind. Adding large amounts of polyunsaturated fats to your diet without removing saturated fats will increase your total fat intake, and, as a consequence, your total caloric intake. This, in turn, can lead to weight gain and obesity. Moreover, polyunsaturated fats are only half as effective at lowering cholesterol levels as saturated fats are at raising them. In other words, you can't eat all the saturated fats you want and then expect to make up for them by piling on the polyunsaturated fat. Another reason to eat polyunsaturated fats in moderation is that although such fats have the positive effect of lowering levels of LDL cholesterol, they may also lower the blood levels of the beneficial HDL cholesterol.

A diet high in monounsaturated fats from olive oil is believed to be responsible for the lower blood cholesterol levels found in people living in Mediterranean countries. The evidence indicated that **monounsaturated fats,** *when substituted for saturated fats in the diet,* **lower total blood cholesterol levels** by lowering LDL cholesterol levels without lowering HDL cholesterol levels.

INTRODUCTION

The total amount of fat in your diet can also affect how your body deals with cholesterol, though its effect is less direct than the effect of saturated fat. A gram of fat provides more than twice as many calories as a gram of protein or carbohydrate. For that reason, a high-fat diet is likely to be a high-calorie diet as well. Any unneeded calories—those that are not burned off—are then stored in the body as fat. Over time, this will lead to weight gain and, eventually, obesity. Gaining weight in itself may raise total blood cholesterol. And, if that weren't enough, a high-fat diet is likely to be high in saturated fats, a condition that further disturbs the body's cholesterol balance.

CHOLESTEROL IN THE DIET

Dietary cholesterol also affects blood cholesterol levels by suppressing the production of LDL receptors. The impact of dietary cholesterol is less than that of saturated fat, however, because of the body's feedback mechanism. This process slows the body's production of cholesterol when large amounts of it are consumed in the diet. But even if your body could adjust its cholesterol balance to accommodate a high-cholesterol diet, the large amount of saturated fat that usually accompanies the cholesterol in food would once again upset the balance. The degree to which dietary cholesterol affects blood cholesterol levels seems to depend on how much total fat and saturated fat are eaten along with it.

The richest source of dietary cholesterol is egg yolks: A single egg yolk contains about 213 milligrams (mg) of cholesterol; as a component of the American diet, eggs contribute more than 35 percent of the total dietary cholesterol. Additional sources of cholesterol that are also rich in saturated fat and total fat include beef, pork, veal, lamb, whole milk, butter, cheese, cream, ice cream, sausages, frankfurters, and most luncheon meats.

Commercially prepared baked goods, processed snack foods, and candy are frequently overlooked sources of large amounts of fat, saturated fat, and cholesterol. These "sweets" are often made with palm oil, coconut oil, or partially hydrogenated vegetable oils because these oils add flavor and are often cheaper than the more costly animal fats. Moreover, many of these products are prepared with eggs.

Be especially careful in fast-food restaurants. Reasonably healthful foods are available, but you may have to search for them. Stay away from cheeseburgers, sausages, most fried foods, and dishes prepared with eggs. Look for foods such as broiled chicken (with the skin removed), plain baked potatoes, and salads with low-fat, low-cholesterol dressings.

IS YOUR BLOOD CHOLESTEROL LEVEL TOO HIGH?
The level of cholesterol in your blood is expressed in milligrams per deciliter (mg/dL), which indicates the amount of cholesterol found in one deciliter of blood. Research has shown that the risk of heart disease increases as the blood cholesterol level rises, especially as it climbs above 200 mg/dL.

INTRODUCTION

In the United States, adults who have a blood cholesterol level of 240 mg/dL or above appear to have more than twice the risk of developing CHD than those with readings below 200 mg/dL. Unfortunately, it has been estimated that more than 100 million Americans have a blood cholesterol level of 200 mg/dL or above. This means about two out of every five people living in the United States fall into this group.

Testing total blood cholesterol

To help you and your physician determine if your blood cholesterol level puts you at high risk for CHD, the National Cholesterol Education Program (NCEP) suggests that all adults aged 20 years or older have a cholesterol test. The NCEP also developed recommendations for classifying cholesterol levels and determining treatment. According to these guidelines, a total blood cholesterol level below 200 mg/dL is considered *desirable* for all adults aged 20 and older. A test result between 200 and 239 mg/dL is regarded as *borderline high*, whereas 240 mg/dL or more is rated as *high*.

Classification Based on Total Blood Cholesterol

<200 mg/dL	desirable
200–239 mg/dL	borderline high
≥240 mg/dL	high

If your blood cholesterol is in the desirable range, you should be given general information on your diet and risk factors, and then advised to have your cholesterol test repeated within five years. You should continue to be careful about your diet to be sure you remain at the desirable level. All test results above 200 should be verified by a second test. This repeat measurement is necessary to confirm the results of the first test and to determine if further treatment is necessary.

If your test places you in the borderline-high range, you may need to be evaluated further with a different test, the lipoprotein analysis. This second test is necessary only if you already have CHD, or you have two or more additional risk factors for the disease.

Other risk factors for the development of CHD include the following:

- Being male
- Cigarette smoking
- High blood pressure (systolic pressure of 140 mm Hg or more, diastolic pressure of 90 mm Hg or more, or both)
- Family history of premature (before the age of 55) CHD
- Low HDL cholesterol level (below 35 mg/dL, confirmed by repeat measurement)
- Advanced hardening of the arteries in the head, legs, feet hands, or arms
- Severe obesity (30 percent or more over ideal bodyweight)

If your total blood cholesterol is in the borderline-high range, you do not have CHD, and you have fewer than two of the other risk factors for CHD, then you should be given information on the *Step One* diet, which is described in the next section. You should have the cholesterol test repeated within one year.

In contrast, if your total blood cholesterol is in the borderline-high range and you have CHD or two or more risk factors for the disease, then you are advised to have an additional test—a lipoprotein analysis—within two months. Those who test in the high range should follow the same advice.

Lipoprotein analysis

A lipoprotein analysis reveals how blood cholesterol is divided between LDL and HDL cholesterol. For an accurate result, this test must be performed twice. If the lipoprotein analysis reveals an LDL cholesterol level below 130 mg/dL, which is considered a desirable range, you can expect to receive general information about diet and risk factors. You will also be advised to have your blood cholesterol tested again within five years.

An LDL cholesterol level between 130 and 159 mg/dL places you in the borderline-high range. If you are in this category, do not have CHD, and have fewer than two of the risk factors mentioned above, then you should be given information on the *Step One* diet and have your cholesterol tested on a yearly basis.

The last category includes those who fall into the borderline-high group who do have CHD or two or more risk factors for CHD. Also in this category is the high-risk group, those who have lipoprotein test results of 160 mg/dL or more. Members of both groups should consider further evaluation by a physician to determine the causes of their high cholesterol.

DIETS TO LOWER BLOOD CHOLESTEROL

The *Step One* diet recommended by the NCEP to lower blood cholesterol levels restricts daily dietary cholesterol intake to less than 300 mg. Total fat is limited to 30 percent of calories, saturated fat to less than 10 percent. No more than 10 percent of total calories should come from polyunsaturated fats. Remaining fat calories in the daily diet should consist of monounsaturated fats.

If the *Step One* diet fails to lower your blood cholesterol to the desirable level, the *Step Two* diet may be recommended. The *Step Two* diet limits daily cholesterol intake to less than 200 mg and saturated fats to less than 7 percent of total calories. The portion of total fat allowed on this plan remains at less than 30 percent, since a diet that is much lower in fat would be difficult for most people to follow. Blood cholesterol can be lowered to satisfactory levels without reducing fat intake any further.

NCEP Dietary Recommendations

	Step One	*Step Two*
Cholesterol	<300 mg	<200 mg
Saturated Fat	<10 percent of total calories	<7 percent of total calories
Total Fat	<30 percent of total calories	<30 percent of total calories

PUTTING YOUR DIET—AND THE COUNTER—TO WORK FOR YOU

The *Step One* diet recommended to help reduce blood cholesterol levels for people in the borderline-high range is actually the same heart-smart diet suggested for all adults, even those with normal cholesterol. It is also advised for children over the age of two. As a basic plan, it is designed to help you and your family eat a nutritious diet that is low in total fat, saturated fat, and cholesterol. Therefore, for most people, even those with blood cholesterol levels in the desirable range of less than 200 mg/dL, the *Step One* diet is appropriate.

As you will see, adopting a heart-healthy diet does not mean depriving yourself of all the foods you love. It simply means making wiser choices in food selection and preparation, eating certain foods only in moderation, and keeping an eye on the overall content of your diet. (The Food Guide Pyramid on pages 28–30 can help you implement these changes.)

To adopt the *Step One* diet, you need to keep track of how much fat and cholesterol you consume each day. That may sound somewhat intimidating, but it doesn't have to be. By simply picking up this book, you've taken the important first step toward cleaning up your diet with a minimum amount of inconvenience. The *Fat Counter Guide* lists the calorie, total fat, saturated fat, and cholesterol content of brand-name and common food items. It also gives the **percentage** of calories from each kind of fat. This way you can make wise food choices when you plan meals and shop for groceries. First, however, you need to look at what the dietary guidelines really mean in terms of the foods you eat, and then learn which foods will fit into your overall dietary plan.

Controlling Fat

Both the *Step One* and the *Step Two* diets place limitations on the amount of total and saturated fat in the diet. Lowering dietary fat has many health benefits. The primary one comes from the fact that saturated fats are the main contributing factor in raising blood cholesterol. Another benefit of a low-fat diet is greater control of body weight, which in turn can help to control blood cholesterol. And a third benefit derives from the link between high-fat diets and certain cancers.

To help you to limit your total fat intake to less than 30 percent of your total calories, this counter specifically lists the *percentages* of calories that come from total and saturated fat for most foods. These percentages are the numbers you need to get your diet into compliance with the NCEP guidelines.

With the information provided in this book, you'll be able to limit your total fat intake. Note that it isn't necessary to eliminate all foods from your diet that derive more than 30 percent of their calories from fat. When you do choose a meal that contains more than the recommended amount of fat, try to balance it out by making lower-fat choices the rest of the day. Keep in mind that you want your *overall* diet to provide less than 30 percent of your total calories from fat.

INTRODUCTION

The same approach works with your intake of saturated fat: Use the values given in this counter for percentages from saturated fat; try to keep your intake within the recommended range of less than ten percent of total calories for the *Step One* diet and less than seven percent for *Step Two*.

Controlling Cholesterol

To limit your dietary cholesterol intake to less than 300 mg per day, you should cut back on foods that are high in cholesterol. Remember, plants do not manufacture cholesterol. So foods that come from plants—cereals, grains, fruits, and vegetables—are cholesterol free. On the other hand, eggs, dairy products, meats, poultry, and fish do come from animal sources and thus do contain cholesterol. Egg yolks are so filled with cholesterol, in fact, that experts recommend no more than three yolks per week, including those used in baked goods, sauces, and pastries.

The *Fat Counter Guide* provides the cholesterol content for hundreds of individual food items. When planning meals, simply add up the cholesterol values shown to find out if the foods you plan to eat fit into your daily cholesterol "budget" of less than 300 mg (or less than 200 mg if you are on the *Step Two* diet). The counter makes it easy to compare similar foods.

AND CONSIDER THIS

Here are some additional tips to help you choose and prepare foods that are low in fat and cholesterol:

- Use low-fat dairy products, such as skim milk, low-fat cottage cheese, nonfat yogurt, and ice milk. Whenever possible, substitute them for whole milk, cream, hard cheese, sour cream, and ice cream.
- Eat poultry and fish more often than meat. When you do choose meat, select only lean cuts. Remove the skin from poultry, and trim away the visible fat from all meat before cooking.
- When buying canned tuna, salmon, or other fish, select products that are packed in water rather than oil.
- Try to limit your daily meat intake to no more than six ounces. Then fill the meals with low-fat foods like vegetables, pasta, and rice.
- Try venison, buffalo, and other wild game animals such as rabbit, pheasant, and duck; they generally contain less fat than domesticated animals bred for their meat.
- Avoid butter and margarine that is made from lard or shortening. As an alternative, use margarine that comes from polyunsaturated oils—corn, safflower, soybean, or sunflower.
- Include plenty of fruits in your diet; they contain no cholesterol and, except for avocados and olives, they are low in fat.
- When preparing meat, fish, or poultry, avoid frying. Bake, roast, or broil them instead. When basting, use wine, lemon juice, or tomato juice rather than fatty drippings.
- Avoid or decrease the consumption of processed luncheon meats and sausages, most of which are high in fat.

INTRODUCTION

- Limit the use of peanut butter and peanut oil.
- Include cereals, breads, pasta, rice, and dried peas and beans frequently in your meals. Not only are they low in saturated fat, they are also high in complex carbohydrates (starch and fiber).
- Commercially prepared baked goods such as pies, cakes, and doughnuts are often high in saturated fat and cholesterol. As an alternative, look for low-fat varieties, or prepare mixes at home with optional no-cholesterol recipes.
- Choose carefully at fast-food restaurants. Salads with low-fat dressing, plain baked potatoes, and broiled chicken without skin or sauce provide healthy alternatives to the usual fat-filled hamburgers and fries.

THE FOOD GUIDE PYRAMID

A healthful diet is the cornerstone of any cholesterol-lowering program. Even in those cases where drugs are prescribed to reduce cholesterol, a diet that is low in saturated fat and cholesterol is still vital.

However, determining which foods fit into this low-fat, low-cholesterol diet can be difficult. That's why the U.S. Department of Agriculture developed the Food Guide Pyramid—to show generally what a healthful diet looks like.

The foundation of a healthful diet is complex carbohydrate, which should provide the bulk of your calories. Breads, cereals, pasta, and so on are low-fat and nutritious food choices. The second level contains the vegetable group and the fruit

FOOD GUIDE PYRAMID

A Guide to Daily Food Choices

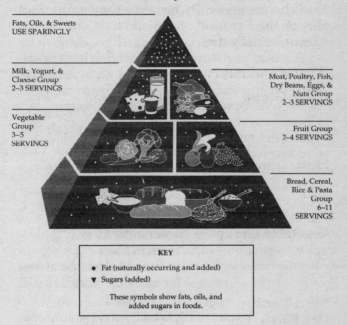

Fats, Oils, & Sweets
USE SPARINGLY

Milk, Yogurt, &
Cheese Group
2–3 SERVINGS

Meat, Poultry, Fish,
Dry Beans, Eggs, &
Nuts Group
2–3 SERVINGS

Vegetable
Group
3–5
SERVINGS

Fruit Group
2–4 SERVINGS

Bread, Cereal,
Rice & Pasta
Group
6–11
SERVINGS

KEY

● Fat (naturally occurring and added)

▼ Sugars (added)

These symbols show fats, oils, and
added sugars in foods.

group; these foods are also virtually fat- and cholesterol free. The dairy group and the meat group
(including legumes, nuts, and eggs) are near the
top not because of their importance, but because
they are to be a smaller proportion of the diet
than the larger, lower levels. Finally, the tip of the
pyramid represents the added sugar and fat in
the diet; these should be used sparingly.

INTRODUCTION

Using the Food Guide Pyramid to plan meals and snacks will help you stick to the *Step One* and even the *Step Two* diet. Let the number of daily servings per group be your guide. If your overall food choices generally have the same proportionality as the Pyramid, you will be on your way to a heart-healthy diet.

What is a serving?

Grain Group	1 slice of bread 1 oz. ready-to-eat cereal ½ cup cooked cereal, rice, or pasta
Fruit Group	1 medium piece of raw fruit ½ cup canned fruit ¾ cup of fruit juice
Vegetable Group	1 cup raw, leafy vegetables ½ cup cut-up vegetables ¾ vegetable juice
Meat, Poultry, Fish, Dry Beans, Eggs, and Nuts Group	2–3 oz. cooked meat, poultry, or fish *May substitute for 1 oz. meat:* ½ cup cooked dry beans 1 egg 2 tbsp. peanut butter
Dairy Group	1 cup milk or yogurt 1½ oz. natural cheese 2 oz. processed cheese

ABOUT THIS COUNTER

This fat counter provides values for hundreds of common foods, identified by brand or generic names, as well as about 200 items from fast-food menus. The data come from the U.S. Department of Agriculture, manufacturers and processors, and directly from food labels.

Separate columns list the calorie (CAL.) and cholesterol (CHOL.) content. Fat is broken down to show amounts of total (TOTAL FAT) and saturated fat (SAT. FAT). Fats are shown in grams (g); milligrams (mg) are used for cholesterol. Percentages of calories are included for both total and saturated fats. These percentages will help those who follow the *Step One* and *Step Two* diets explained earlier in the introduction. In addition, the percentage figures provide a particularly useful guide to fat content because the percentage of fat in a given item doesn't change, regardless of the portion size. For example, look up peanut butter in the counter. You will find that between 76 and 81 percent of its calories come from fat. This will be consistent whether you eat a spoonful or the entire jar.

With a simple formula, you can calculate the percentages for foods not included on our list: Multiply grams of fat (or saturated fat) times 9, divide the result by the total number of calories, then multiply your answer by 100. This gives the percentage of total calories that come from fat (or saturated fat). For example, one raw egg contains 6 grams of fat and has 80 calories. Using the formula, multiply 6 by 9 to get 54; divide 54 by 80 to get 0.675; and multiply 0.675 by 100 to get 67.5 percent (which is then rounded off to 68 percent). Thus, 68 percent of the calories in one raw egg comes from fat.

Foods on the list are grouped into common categories, like "Beverages" and "Poultry," which are arranged in alphabetical order. After a brief description of each item, a specific portion size is given. The values in each column pertain to the portion size listed.

When trace amounts are shown for fat or saturated fat, it is impossible to calculate exact percentages, so "na" is used. However, as a practical matter, if only trace amounts of these elements are present, the percentage of calories they provide is generally quite low, usually less than ten percent.

The symbol "<" means "less than," so "<1" indicates the presence of less than one unit of whatever is being measured (less than one percent, less than one gram). All of the fractional amounts have been rounded off.

Finally, while every effort has been made to ensure that the values listed are as accurate as possible, they are subject to change as food manufacturers modify the ingredients and methods of preparation.

Baked Goods

FOOD/PORTION SIZE	CAL.	FAT Total (g)	FAT As % of Cal.	SAT. FAT Total (g)	SAT. FAT As % of Cal.	CHOL. (mg)
CAKE						
Angel Food Cake Mix, Duncan Hines, 1/12 of cake (36 g)	140	0	0	0	0	0
Chocolate Loaf, Fat & Cholesterol Free, Entenmann's, 1/5 of cake (85 g)	210	0	0	0	0	0
Coffeecake, Butter Streusel, Sara Lee, 1/6 of cake (54 g)	220	12	49	6	25	35
Cupcakes Lights, Hostess, 2 cakes (77 g)	240	<3	9	<1	2	0
Devil's Food Cake Mix, Moist Deluxe, Duncan Hines, 1/12 of cake, regular recipe (43 g)	290	15	47	3	9	45
Same as above, no-cholesterol recipe	280	15	48	2	6	0
Gingerbread Cake & Cookie Mix, Betty Crocker, 1/9 of cake (1.6 oz.), regular recipe	220	7	29	2	8	30
Same as above, no-cholesterol recipe	210	6	26	0	0	0
Orange Supreme Cake Mix, Duncan Hines, 1/12 of cake, regular recipe (43 g)	250	11	40	2	7	45
Same as above, no-cholesterol recipe	240	10	38	<2	6	0
Pound Cake, All-Butter, Sara Lee, 1/6 piece (76 g)	310	17	49	9	26	75
Pound Cake, Free & Light, Sara Lee, 1/4 piece (71 g)	200	4	18	1	5	0
Twinkies Lights, Low Fat, Hostess, 2 cakes (77 g)	230	<3	10	<1	2	0

BAKED GOODS

FOOD/PORTION SIZE	CAL.	FAT Total (g)	FAT As % of Cal.	SAT. FAT Total (g)	SAT. FAT As % of Cal.	CHOL. (mg)
White Cake Mix, Pillsbury Plus, 1/10 of cake (52 g)	220	5	20	2	8	0
White Cake Mix, Moist Deluxe, Duncan Hines, regular recipe, 1/12 of cake (43 g)	240	10	38	2	8	45
Same as above, no-cholesterol recipe	250	12	43	<3	9	0
Yellow Cake Mix, Lovin' Lites, Pillsbury (using egg whites), 1/12 of cake	170	3	16	1	5	0
Yellow Cake Mix, Super Moist Light, Betty Crocker, regular recipe, 1/10 pkg. (52 g mix)	230	<5	18	2	8	65
Same as above, no-cholesterol recipe	210	3	13	<2	6	0
COOKIES						
Chocolate Chip, Chips Ahoy, Nabisco, 3 cookies (32 g)	160	8	45	<3	14	0
Chocolate chip, refrigerated dough, 1 cookie	56	3	48	1	16	6
Fig Newtons, Fat Free, Nabisco, 2 cookies (29 g)	100	0	0	0	0	0
Oatmeal Raisin, Fat & Cholesterol Free, Entenmann's, 2 cookies (24 g)	80	0	0	0	0	0
Oreos, Nabisco, 3 cookies (33 g)	160	7	39	<2	8	0
Oreos, Reduced Fat, Nabisco, 3 cookies (32 g)	140	5	32	1	6	0
Sandwich (chocolate or shortbread, commercial), 1 small cookie	39	2	46	1	23	7
Sugar, refrigerated dough, 1 cookie	59	3	46	1	15	7

FOOD/PORTION SIZE	CAL.	FAT Total (g)	FAT As % of Cal.	SAT. FAT Total (g)	SAT. FAT As % of Cal.	CHOL. (mg)
Teddy Grahams Bearwiches, Cinnamon, Nabisco, 24 pieces (30 g)	140	4	26	1	6	0
Wafers, vanilla, 5 cookies	93	4	39	1	10	13
PASTRY						
Coffeecake, Easy Mix, Aunt Jemima, ⅛ of cake	170	5	26	na	na	na
Danish, fruit, 4¼-in. round, 1 pastry	235	13	50	4	15	56
Danish, plain, 4¼-in. round, 1 pastry	220	12	49	4	16	49
Toaster, 1 pastry	210	6	26	2	9	0
PIE						
(All pies include crust made with enriched flour and vegetable shortening.)						
Apple, ⅙ of 9-in. pie	405	18	40	5	11	0
Apple, Homestyle, Sara Lee, ⅛ of pie (131 g)	330	17	46	<4	10	0
Blueberry, ⅙ of 9-in. pie	380	17	40	4	9	0
Cherry, ⅙ of 9-in. pie	410	18	40	5	11	0
Lemon meringue, ⅙ of 9-in. pie	355	14	35	4	10	143
Peach, ⅙ of 9-in. pie	405	17	38	4	9	0
Pecan, ⅙ of 9-in. pie	575	32	50	5	8	95
Piecrust, Graham Cracker, Keebler, ¹⁄₁₀ crust (26 g)	130	6	42	<2	10	0
Piecrust, mix, 9-in., 2-crust pie	1485	93	56	23	14	0
Piecrust, Pet Ritz, ⅛ of 9-in. crust (18 g)	80	5	56	2	23	5
Pumpkin, ⅙ of 9-in. pie	320	17	48	6	17	109

BAKED GOODS

FOOD/PORTION SIZE	CAL.	FAT Total (g)	FAT As % of Cal.	SAT. FAT Total (g)	SAT. FAT As % of Cal.	CHOL. (mg)
MISCELLANEOUS						
Brownie Mix, Fudge, Betty Crocker, 1 brownie (34 g mix) as baked	200	9	41	2	9	25
Brownie Mix, Fudge, Lovin' Lites, Pillsbury, 1/16 pkg. (35 g) as baked	160	<4	20	1	6	15
Brownie Mix, Fudge, Low Fat, Betty Crocker, 1 brownie (35 g mix)	130	<3	17	<1	3	0
Doughnuts, cake, plain, 1 doughnut	210	12	51	3	13	20
Doughnuts, yeast, glazed, 1 doughnut	192	13	61	5	23	29
Pizza Crust, All Ready, Pillsbury, 1/4 crust (71 g)	190	<3	12	<1	2	0
Pizza Crust, Boboli, 1/8 shell (57 g)	150	<4	21	1	6	5

Baking Products & Condiments

FOOD/PORTION SIZE	CAL.	FAT Total (g)	FAT As % of Cal.	SAT. FAT Total (g)	SAT. FAT As % of Cal.	CHOL. (mg)
Bacos, 1 tbsp. (7 g)	30	1	30	0	0	0
Baking Powder, Clabber Girl, 1/4 tsp. (1.1 g)	0	0	0	0	0	0
Baking soda for home use, 1 tsp.	5	0	0	0	0	0
Barbecue Sauce, Original, Open Pit, 2 tbsp. (30 mL)	50	<1	9	0	0	0
Barbecue sauce, ready to serve, 1 tbsp.	10	tr	na	tr	na	0

BAKING PRODUCTS & CONDIMENTS

FOOD/PORTION SIZE	CAL.	FAT Total (g)	FAT As % of Cal.	SAT. FAT Total (g)	SAT. FAT As % of Cal.	CHOL. (mg)
Barbecue Sauce, Thick 'n' Spicy, Kraft, 2 tbsp. (34 g)	50	0	0	0	0	0
Barley, pearled, light, uncooked, 1 cup	700	2	3	<1	tr	0
Bulgur, uncooked, 1 cup	600	3	5	1	2	0
Butterscotch Topping, Smucker's, 2 tbsp. (41 g)	130	0	0	0	0	0
Caramel Topping, Kraft, 2 tbsp. (41 g)	120	0	0	0	0	0
Catsup, 1 tbsp.	15	tr	na	tr	na	0
Catsup, Weight Watchers, 1 tbsp.	12	0	0	0	0	0
Celery seed, 1 tsp.	10	1	90	tr	na	0
Chili powder, 1 tsp.	10	tr	na	<1	na	0
Chocolate, Semi-Sweet, Baker's, 1 square (28 g)	130	9	62	5	35	0
Chocolate, Unsweetened Chocolate Baking Bar, Baker's, 1 square (28 g)	140	14	90	9	58	0
Chocolate Chips, Real, Semi-Sweet, Baker's, 2 tbsp. (15 g)	70	4	51	<3	32	0
Chocolate Chips, Semi-Sweet, Hershey's, ¼ cup	220	12	49	7	29	8
Chocolate Flavored Chips, Semi-Sweet, Baker's, ¼ cup	200	9	41	7	29	0
Chocolate Flavored Topping, Kraft, 2 tbsp.	120	0	0	0	0	0
Chocolate Topping, Kraft, 1 tbsp.	50	0	0	0	0	0
Cinnamon, 1 tsp.	5	tr	na	tr	na	0
Cocktail Sauce, Sauceworks, Kraft, 1 tbsp.	14	0	0	0	0	0
Cocoa Powder, Hershey's, 1 tbsp. (5 g)	20	<1	23	0	0	0

BAKING PRODUCTS & CONDIMENTS

FOOD/PORTION SIZE	CAL.	FAT Total (g)	FAT As % of Cal.	SAT. FAT Total (g)	SAT. FAT As % of Cal.	CHOL. (mg)
Coconut, Angel Flake, Baker's (bag), ⅓ cup	115	8	63	8	63	0
Coconut, Premium Shred, Baker's, ⅓ cup	140	9	58	9	58	0
Cornmeal, degermed, enriched, dry, 1 cup	500	2	4	<1	na	0
Cornmeal, whole-ground, unbolted, dry, 1 cup	435	5	10	<1	na	0
Curry powder, 1 tsp.	5	tr	na	na	na	0
Flour, buckwheat, light, sifted, 1 cup	340	1	3	<1	na	0
Flour, cake/pastry, enriched, sifted, spooned, 1 cup	350	1	3	<1	na	0
Flour, self-rising, enriched, unsifted, spooned, 1 cup	440	1	2	<1	na	0
Flour, wheat, all-purpose, sifted, spooned, 1 cup	420	1	2	<1	na	0
Flour, wheat, all-purpose, unsifted, spooned, 1 cup	455	1	2	<1	na	0
Flour, whole-wheat from hard wheats, stirred, 1 cup	400	2	5	<1	na	0
Frosting, Chocolate-flavored, Creamy Deluxe, Betty Crocker, 2 tbsp. (36 g)	140	6	39	<2	10	0
Frosting, Chocolate Fudge, Frosting Supreme, Pillsbury, 2 tbsp. (34 g)	140	6	39	<2	10	0
Frosting, Cream Cheese, Creamy Homestyle, Duncan Hines, 2 tbsp. (32 g)	140	5	32	<2	10	0
Garlic powder, 1 tsp.	10	tr	na	tr	na	0
Honey, strained or extracted, 1 tbsp.	65	0	0	0	0	0
Horseradish, Cream Style, Prepared, Kraft, 1 tbsp.	12	1	75	0	0	0
Horseradish, Prepared, Kraft, 1 tbsp.	10	0	0	0	0	0

BAKING PRODUCTS & CONDIMENTS

FOOD/PORTION SIZE	CAL.	FAT Total (g)	FAT As % of Cal.	SAT. FAT Total (g)	SAT. FAT As % of Cal.	CHOL. (mg)
Horseradish, Sauce, Kraft, 1 tsp. (5 g)	20	<2	68	0	0	<5
Hot Fudge, Light Topping, Smucker's, 2 tbsp (39 g)	90	0	0	0	0	0
Hot Fudge Topping, Kraft, 2 tbsp. (41 g)	140	4	26	2	13	0
Jams and preserves, 1 tbsp.	55	tr	na	0	0	0
Jam, Strawberry, Smucker's, 1 tbsp. (20 g)	60	0	0	0	0	0
Jellies, 1 tbsp.	50	tr	na	tr	na	0
Marshmallow Creme, Kraft, 2 tbsp. (12 g)	40	0	0	0	0	0
Mayonnaise, Cholesterol Free, Reduced Fat, Hellmann's, 1 tbsp. (16 g)	40	3	68	<1	11	0
Mayonnaise, Hellmann's, 1 tbsp. (14 g)	100	11	99	<2	14	5
Mayonnaise, Light, Reduced Calorie, Kraft, 1 tbsp. (15 g)	50	5	90	1	10	5
Mayonnaise, Nonfat, Kraft Free, 1 tbsp. (16 g)	10	0	0	0	0	0
Mayonnaise, Real, Kraft, 1 tbsp. (14 g)	100	11	99	2	18	10
Molasses, Grandma's, 1 tbsp. (15 mL)	50	0	0	0	0	0
Mustard, Country Dijon, Grey Poupon, 1 tsp. (5 g)	5	0	0	0	0	0
Mustard, French's, Classic Yellow, 1 tsp. (15 g)	0	0	0	0	0	0
Mustard, prepared yellow, 1 tsp. or individual packet	5	tr	na	tr	na	0
Onion powder, 1 tsp.	5	tr	na	tr	na	0
Oregano, 1 tsp.	5	tr	na	tr	na	0
Paprika, 1 tsp.	6	tr	na	tr	na	0
Pepper, ground, black, 1 tsp.	5	tr	na	tr	na	0

BAKING PRODUCTS & CONDIMENTS

FOOD/PORTION SIZE	CAL.	FAT Total (g)	FAT As % of Cal.	SAT. FAT Total (g)	SAT. FAT As % of Cal.	CHOL. (mg)
Picante Sauce, Medium, Pace, 2 tbsp. (31.5 g)	10	0	0	0	0	0
Pineapple Topping, Smucker's, 2 tbsp. (40 g)	110	0	0	0	0	0
Preserves, Apricot, Knott's Berry Farm, 1 tbsp. (20 g)	50	0	0	0	0	0
Salad Dressing, Light, Miracle Whip, 1 tbsp. (15 g)	40	3	68	0	0	0
Salad Dressing, Miracle Whip, 1 tbsp. (14 g)	70	7	90	1	13	5
Salsa, Thick & Chunky, Mild, Ortega, 1 tbsp.	4	0	0	0	0	0
Salt, 1 tsp.	0	0	0	0	0	0
Sandwich Spread, Kraft, 1 tbsp. (15 g)	50	5	90	<1	9	5
Seasoning Blend, Mrs. Dash, 1 tsp.	12	0	0	0	0	0
Seasoning Mixture, Original Recipe for Chicken, Shake 'N Bake, ¼ pouch	80	tr	na	tr	na	0
Shrimp Sauce, Hoffman House, 2 tbsp. (30 g)	60	2	30	0	0	0
Soy sauce, ready to serve, 1 tbsp.	11	0	0	0	0	0
Strawberry Topping, Kraft, 2 tbsp.	110	0	0	0	0	0
Sugar, brown, packed, 1 cup	820	0	0	0	0	0
Sugar, powdered, sifted, spooned into cup, 1 cup	385	0	0	0	0	0
Sugar, white granulated, 1 cup	770	0	0	0	0	0
Sweet 'n Sour Sauce, Kraft Sauceworks, 2 tbsp. (35 g)	60	0	0	0	0	0

BAKING PRODUCTS & CONDIMENTS

FOOD/PORTION SIZE	CAL.	FAT Total (g)	FAT As % of Cal.	SAT. FAT Total (g)	SAT. FAT As % of Cal.	CHOL. (mg)
Syrup, chocolate-flavored syrup or topping, fudge type, 2 tbsp.	125	5	36	3	22	0
Syrup, chocolate-flavored syrup or topping, thin type, 2 tbsp.	85	tr	na	<1	na	0
Syrup, molasses, cane, blackstrap, 2 tbsp.	85	0	0	0	0	0
Syrup, Regular, Log Cabin, ¼ cup (59 mL)	200	0	0	0	0	0
Syrup, table (corn & maple), 2 tbsp.	122	0	0	0	0	0
Tabasco Sauce, 1 tsp. (5 g)	0	0	0	0	0	0
Tartar sauce, 1 tbsp.	75	8	96	1	12	4
Tartar Sauce, Fat Free, Cholesterol Free, Nonfat, Kraft, 2 tbsp. (32 g)	25	0	0	0	0	0
Tartar Sauce, Hellmann's, 1 tbsp. (14 g)	70	8	100	1	13	5
Tartar Sauce, Natural Lemon Herb Flavor, Sauceworks, 2 tbsp. (28 g)	150	16	96	<3	15	15
Vinegar, Apple Cider, Heinz, ½ fl. oz.	2	0	0	0	0	0
Vinegar, Cider, Heinz, 2 tbsp.	4	0	0	0	0	0
Vinegar, Wine, Red or White, Heinz, 2 tbsp.	4	0	0	0	0	0
Worcestershire Sauce, Heinz, 1 tsp. (5 mL)	0	0	0	0	0	0
Yeast, baker's dry active, 1 pkg.	20	tr	na	tr	na	0
Yeast, brewer's dry, 1 tbsp.	25	tr	na	tr	na	0

Beverages

FOOD/PORTION SIZE	CAL.	FAT Total (g)	FAT As % of Cal.	SAT. FAT† Total (g)	SAT. FAT† As % of Cal.	CHOL. (mg)
ALCOHOL						
Beer, light, 12 fl. oz.	95	0	0	0	0	0
Beer, regular, 12 fl. oz.	150	0	0	0	0	0
Gin, rum, vodka, whiskey, 80 proof, 1½ fl. oz.	97	0	0	0	0	0
Gin, rum, vodka, whiskey, 90 proof, 1½ fl. oz.	110	0	0	0	0	0
Wine, table, red, 3½ fl. oz.	74	0	0	0	0	0
Wine, table, white, 3½ fl. oz.	70	0	0	0	0	0
COFFEE						
Brewed, 6 fl. oz.	tr	tr	na	tr	na	0
Cafe Francais, General Foods International Coffees, 6 fl. oz.	50	3	54	0	0	0
Coffee Flavor Instant Hot Beverage, Postum, 6 fl. oz.	12	0	0	0	0	0
Instant, Folger's, 1 tbsp.	8	0	0	0	0	0
Instant, prepared, 6 fl.oz.	tr	tr	na	tr	na	0
Swiss Mocha, General Foods Sugar Free International Coffees, 6 fl. oz.	30	2	51	0	0	0
JUICE						
Apple, bottled or canned, 1 cup	115	tr	na	tr	na	0
Apple Berry Burst, Dole, 8 fl. oz. (240 mL)	120	0	0	0	0	0
Apple, Pure 100%, Mott's, 8 fl. oz. (240 mL)	120	0	0	0	0	0
Cherry, Mountain, Pure & Light, Dole, 6 fl. oz.	100	0	0	0	0	0
Cherry, Pure & Light, Dole, ¾ cup	90	0	0	0	0	0

FOOD/PORTION SIZE	CAL.	FAT Total (g)	FAT As % of Cal.	SAT. FAT Total (g)	SAT. FAT As % of Cal.	CHOL. (mg)
Cranberry Juice Cocktail, Ocean Spray, 8 fl. oz. (240 mL)	140	0	0	0	0	0
Grape, canned or bottled, 1 cup	155	tr	na	<1	<1	0
Grape, frozen concentrate, sweetened, diluted, 1 cup	125	tr	na	<1	<1	0
Grapefruit, canned, sweetened, 1 cup	115	tr	na	tr	na	0
Grapefruit, canned, unsweetened, 1 cup	95	tr	na	tr	na	0
Grapefruit, Ocean Spray, 8 fl. oz. (240 mL)	100	0	0	0	0	0
Grapefruit, raw, 1 cup	95	tr	na	tr	na	0
Lemon, canned or bottled, unsweetened, 1 oup	50	1	18	<1	2	0
Lemon, raw, 1 cup	60	tr	na	tr	na	0
Lemon-Lime, Gatorade, 8 fl. oz. (240 mL)	50	0	0	0	0	0
Lemon, ReaLemon Juice from Concentrate, Borden, 1 tsp. (5 mL)	0	0	0	0	0	0
Lime, canned or bottled, unsweetened, 1 cup	50	1	18	<1	2	0
Lime, raw, 1 cup	65	tr	na	tr	na	0
Orange, canned, unsweetened, 1 cup	105	tr	na	tr	na	0
Orange, chilled, 1 cup	110	1	8	<1	<1	0
Orange, frozen concentrate, diluted, 1 cup	110	tr	na	tr	na	0
Orange, raw, 1 cup	110	tr	na	<1	<1	0
Orange and grapefruit, canned, 1 cup	105	tr	na	tr	na	0
Peach, Orchard Peach, Dole, 8 fl. oz. (240 mL)	140	0	0	0	0	0

BEVERAGES

FOOD/PORTION SIZE	CAL.	FAT Total (g)	FAT As % of Cal.	SAT. FAT Total (g)	SAT. FAT As % of Cal.	CHOL. (mg)
Pineapple, Canned, Dole, 6 fl. oz.	100	0	0	0	0	0
Pineapple/Orange Fruit Blends, Del Monte, approx. 8 fl. oz. (240 mL)	130	0	0	0	0	0
Pineapple Passion Banana, Dole, 8 fl. oz. (240 mL)	120	0	0	0	0	0
Pineapple, unsweetened, canned, 1 cup	140	tr	na	tr	na	0
Prune, Sunsweet, 8 fl. oz. (240 mL)	180	0	0	0	0	0
Tomato, canned, 1 cup	40	tr	na	tr	na	0
Vegetable Juice, V-8, 8 fl. oz. (240 mL)	50	0	0	0	0	0
MILK						
Buttermilk, 1 cup	100	2	18	1	9	9
Canned, condensed, sweetened, 1 cup	980	27	25	17	16	104
Canned, evaporated, skim, 1 cup	200	1	5	<1	1	9
Canned, evaporated, whole, 1 cup	340	19	50	12	32	74
Chocolate, low fat (1%), 1 cup	160	3	17	2	11	7
Chocolate, low fat (2%), 1 cup	180	5	25	3	15	17
Chocolate Malt Flavor, Ovaltine Classic, ¾ oz.	80	0	0	0	0	0
Cocoa Mix, Milk Chocolate, Carnation, 1 envelope	110	1	8	tr	na	1
Cocoa Mix, Rich Chocolate, Carnation, 1 envelope	110	1	8	1	8	1
Dried, nonfat, instant, 1 cup	245	tr	na	<1	1	12
Dried, nonfat, instant, 1 envelope (3⅕ oz.) (makes 1 quart)	325	1	3	<1	1	17

FOOD/PORTION SIZE	CAL.	FAT Total (g)	FAT As % of Cal.	SAT. FAT Total (g)	SAT. FAT As % of Cal.	CHOL. (mg)
Eggnog (commercial), 1 cup	340	19	50	11	29	149
Evaporated Filled Milk, Milnot, 2 tbsp. (30 mL)	40	2	45	0	0	0
Evaporated Milk, Pet, 2 tbsp.	43	3	63	2	42	9
Evaporated Skim Milk, Light, Pet, 2 tbsp. (30 mL)	25	0	0	0	0	5
Evaporated Skim Milk, Lite, Carnation, 2 tbsp.	25	0	0	0	0	3
Low fat (2%), milk solids added, 1 cup	125	5	36	3	22	18
Low fat (2%), no milk solids, 1 cup	120	5	38	3	23	18
Malted, chocolate, powder, ¾ oz.	84	1	11	<1	5	1
Malted, chocolate, powder, prepared with 8 oz. whole milk	235	9	34	6	23	34
Malt Flavor, Classic, Ovaltine, ¾ oz.	80	tr	na	tr	na	0
Nonfat (skim), milk solids added, 1 cup	90	1	10	<1	4	5
Nonfat (skim), no milk solids, 1 cup	85	tr	na	<1	3	4
Quik, Chocolate, Nestlé, 2 tbsp. (22 g)	90	<1	5	<1	5	0
Shake Mix, Alba 77 Fit n' Frosty, all flavors, 1 envelope	70	0	0	0	0	3
Skim Milk, Fortified, Lite-line or Viva, Borden, 1 cup	100	1	9	tr	na	5
Whole (3.3% fat), 1 cup	150	8	48	5	30	33
SOFT DRINKS, CARBONATED						
7-Up, 1 can (335 mL)	160	0	0	0	0	0
7-Up, Diet, 1 can	0	0	0	0	0	0

BEVERAGES

FOOD/PORTION SIZE	CAL.	FAT Total (g)	FAT As % of Cal.	SAT. FAT Total (g)	SAT. FAT As % of Cal.	CHOL. (mg)
Bitter Lemon, Schweppes, 10 fl. oz. (300 mL)	140	0	0	0	0	0
Cherry Coke, Coca-Cola, 1 can	150	0	0	0	0	0
Club soda, 6 fl. oz.	0	0	0	0	0	0
Coca-Cola Classic, 1 can	140	0	0	0	0	0
Diet Coke, 1 can	0	0	0	0	0	0
Diet Coke, Caffeine Free, 1 can	0	0	0	0	0	0
Diet Dr. Pepper, 1 can	0	0	0	0	0	0
Diet Pepsi, 1 can	0	0	0	0	0	0
Diet Pepsi, Caffeine Free, 1 can	0	0	0	0	0	0
Diet-Rite, Cola, 1 can	0	0	0	0	0	0
Diet-Rite, Cranberry, 1 can	0	0	0	0	0	0
Fresca, 1 can	0	0	0	0	0	0
Ginger Ale, Schweppes, 8 fl. oz. (240 mL)	90	0	0	0	0	0
Grape, carbonated, 6 fl. oz.	90	0	0	0	0	0
Orange, carbonated, 6 fl. oz.	90	0	0	0	0	0
Pepsi-Cola, Caffeine-Free, 1 can	150	0	0	0	0	0
Root beer, 6 fl. oz.	83	0	0	0	0	0
Root Beer, Dad's, Diet, 1 can	0	0	0	0	0	0
SOFT DRINKS, NONCARBONATED						
Country Time Drink Mix, Sugar Sweetened, Lemonade/Pink Lemonade, mix for 8 fl. oz. (18 g)	70	0	0	0	0	0
Country Time Sugar Free Drink Mix, Lemonade/Pink Lemonade, 8 fl. oz. ⅛ tub (1.9 g)	5	0	0	0	0	0

FOOD/PORTION SIZE	CAL.	FAT Total (g)	FAT As % of Cal.	SAT. FAT Total (g)	SAT. FAT As % of Cal.	CHOL. (mg)
Country Time Sugar Free Drink Mix, Lemon-Lime, 8 fl. oz. ⅛ tub (1.9 g)	5	0	0	0	0	0
Crystal Light Sugar Free Drink Mix, all flavors, 8 fl. oz. (1.7 g)	5	0	0	0	0	0
Grape drink, noncarbonated, canned, 6 fl. oz.	100	0	0	0	0	0
Hi-C Cherry Drink, 8.45 fl. oz.	140	0	0	0	0	0
Hi-C Citrus Cooler Drink, 8 fl. oz. (240 mL)	130	0	0	0	0	0
Hi-C Double Fruit Cooler Drink, 6 oz.	90	0	0	0	0	0
Hi-C Fruit Punch Drink, 8 fl. oz.(240 mL)	130	0	0	0	0	0
Hi-C Hula Punch Drink, 8.45 oz.	120	0	0	0	0	0
Kool-Aid Koolers Juice Drink, all flavors, 1 bottle (200 mL)	100	0	0	0	0	0
Kool-Aid Soft Drink Mix, Sugar-Sweetened, all flavors, 8 fl. oz. (17 g)	60	0	0	0	0	0
Kool-Aid Soft Drink Mix, Unsweetened, all flavors, 8 fl. oz. (0.6 g)	0	0	0	0	0	0
Kool-Aid Sugar-Free Soft Drink Mix, all flavors, 8 fl. oz. (1.1 g)	5	0	0	0	0	0
Lemonade concentrate, frozen, diluted, 6 fl. oz.	80	tr	na	tr	na	0
Limeade concentrate, frozen, diluted, 6 fl. oz.	75	tr	na	tr	na	0
Ocean Spray, Cran-Apple Drink, 8 fl. oz. (240 mL)	160	0	0	0	0	0

BEVERAGES

FOOD/PORTION SIZE	CAL.	FAT Total (g)	FAT As % of Cal.	SAT. FAT Total (g)	SAT. FAT As % of Cal.	CHOL. (mg)
Ocean Spray, Cran-Grape Drink, 8 fl. oz. (240 mL)	150	0	0	0	0	0
Ocean Spray, Cran-Raspberry Drink, 8 fl. oz. (240 mL)	140	0	0	0	0	0
Pineapple-grapefruit juice drink, 6 fl. oz.	90	tr	na	0	0	0
Wyler's Punch Mix, Sweetened, all flavors, 8 fl. oz.	90	0	0	0	0	0
Wyler's Punch Mix, Unsweetened, all flavors, 8 fl. oz. (0.6 g)	0	0	0	0	0	0

TEA

FOOD/PORTION SIZE	CAL.	FAT Total (g)	FAT As % of Cal.	SAT. FAT Total (g)	SAT. FAT As % of Cal.	CHOL. (mg)
Berry, Crystal Light Fruit-Tea Sugar Free Drink Mix, 8 fl. oz. (1.2 g)	5	0	0	0	0	0
Brewed, Lipton, 8 fl. oz.	3	tr	na	0	0	0
Citrus, Crystal Light Fruit-Tea Sugar Free Drink Mix, 8 fl. oz. (2 g)	5	0	0	0	0	0
Iced Tea, Crystal Light Sugar Free Drink Mix, 8 fl. oz. (1.1 g)	5	0	0	0	0	0
Instant, powder, sweetened, 8 fl. oz.	85	tr	na	tr	na	0
Instant, powder, unsweetened, 8 fl.oz.	tr	tr	na	tr	na	0
Natural Brew, Crystal Light Fruit-Tea Sugar Free Drink Mix, 8 fl. oz.	4	0	0	0	0	0
Tropical Fruit Punch, Crystal Light Fruit-Tea Sugar Free Drink Mix, 8 fl. oz. (1.2 g)	5	0	0	0	0	0

Breads & Cereals

FOOD/PORTION SIZE	CAL.	FAT Total (g)	FAT As % of Cal.	SAT. FAT Total (g)	SAT. FAT As % of Cal.	CHOL. (mg)
BISCUITS						
Baking powder, home recipe, 1 biscuit	100	5	45	1	9	tr
Baking powder, refrigerated dough, 1 biscuit	65	2	28	1	14	1
BREAD						
Boston brown, canned, 3¼ x ¼-in. slice	95	1	9	<1	3	3
Cracked-wheat, 1 slice	65	1	14	<1	3	0
Crumbs, enriched, dry, grated, 1 cup	390	5	12	2	5	5
Crumbs. white, enriched, soft, 1 cup	120	2	15	<1	5	0
French, enriched, 5 x 2¼ x 1-in. slice	100	1	9	<1	3	0
Frozen Bread Dough, Texas White Roll, Rhodes, 1 roll (38 g)	100	2	18	0	0	0
Frozen Bread Dough, Texas Whole Wheat, Rhodes, 2 oz.	129	1	7	tr	<1	0
Italian, enriched, 4½ x 3¼ x ¾-in. slice	85	tr	na	tr	na	0
Oat, Hearty Slices Crunchy Oat Bread, Pepperidge Farm, 1 slice, (38 g, 1.4 oz.)	100	2	18	0	0	0
Oat, Oat Bran Bread, Roman Meal, 1 slice (28 g)	70	1	13	0	0	0
Pita, enriched, white, 6-in. diameter, 1 pita	165	1	5	<1	<1	0
Pumpernickel, ⅔ rye, ⅓ wheat, 1 slice	80	1	11	<1	2	0
Raisin, enriched, 1 slice	65	1	14	<1	3	0
Rye, ⅔ wheat, ⅓ rye, 4¾ x 3¾ x 7/16-in. slice	65	1	14	<1	3	0

BREADS & CEREALS

FOOD/PORTION SIZE	CAL.	FAT Total (g)	FAT As % of Cal.	SAT. FAT Total (g)	SAT. FAT As % of Cal.	CHOL. (mg)
Vienna, enriched, 4¾ x 4 x ½-in. slice	70	1	13	<1	3	0
Wheat, Soft, Brownberry, 2 slices (43 g)	80	1	11	0	0	0
Wheat, Stoneground 100% Wheat, Wonder, 1 slice	70	1	13	na	na	0
White, Country White Hearty Slices, Pepperidge Farm, 1 slice (38 g, 1.4 oz.)	90	1	10	0	0	0
White, Home Pride Buttertop, 1 slice (27 g)	70	1	13	0	0	0
White, Wonder, 2 slices (49 g)	120	<2	11	0	0	0
Whole-wheat, 16-slice loaf, 1 slice	70	1	13	<1	5	0
CEREALS, COLD						
40% Bran Flakes, Post, ⅔ cup (1 oz.)	90	tr	na	tr	na	0
100% Bran, Nabisco, ⅓ cup (1 oz.)	70	1	13	tr	na	0
100% Natural, Oats & Honey, Quaker, ½ cup (48 g)	220	8	33	<4	14	0
All-Bran, Kellogg's, ½ cup (30 g, 1.1 oz.)	80	1	11	0	0	0
Alpha-Bits, Post, 1 cup (32 g)	130	1	7	0	0	0
Apple Jacks, Kellogg's, 1 cup (30 g, 1.1 oz.)	110	0	0	0	0	0
Cap'n Crunch, Quaker, ¾ cup (27 g)	110	<2	12	0	0	0
Cap'n Crunch Peanut Butter, Quaker, ¾ cup (27 g)	120	3	23	1	8	0

FOOD/PORTION SIZE	CAL.	FAT Total (g)	FAT As % of Cal.	SAT. FAT Total (g)	SAT. FAT As % of Cal.	CHOL. (mg)
Cheerios, General Mills, 1 cup (30 g)	110	2	16	0	0	0
Cheerios, Honey-Nut, General Mills, 1 cup (30 g)	120	<2	11	0	0	0
Cocoa Krispies, Kellogg's, ¾ cup (30 g, 1.1 oz.)	110	0	0	0	0	0
Cocoa Pebbles, Post, ¾ cup (29 g)	120	1	8	1	8	0
Cocoa Puffs, General Mills, 1 cup (30 g)	120	1	8	0	0	0
Common Sense Oat Bran, Kellogg's, ¾ cup (30 g, 1.1 oz.)	110	1	8	0	0	0
Complete Bran Flakes, Kellogg's, 1 cup (30 g, 1.1 oz.)	100	<1	5	0	0	0
Corn Chex, Ralston Purina, 1¼ cups (30 g)	100	0	0	0	0	0
Corn Flakes, Kellogg's, 1 cup (28 g, 1 oz.)	100	0	0	0	0	0
Corn Flakes, Post Toasties, 1 cup (28 g)	100	0	0	0	0	0
Corn Flakes, Total, ¾ cup (30 g)	100	<1	5	0	0	0
Cracklin' Oat Bran, Kellogg's, ¾ cup (55 g, 2 oz.)	230	8	31	3	12	0
Crispy Wheats & Raisins, 1 cup (55 g)	190	1	5	0	0	0
Froot Loops, Kellogg's, 1 cup (30 g, 1.1 oz.)	120	1	8	0	0	0
Frosted Flakes, Kellogg's, ¾ cup (30 g, 1.1 oz.)	120	0	0	0	0	0
Frosted Mini-Wheats, Kellogg's, 1 cup (55 g, 2 oz.)	190	1	5	0	0	0

BREADS & CEREALS

FOOD/PORTION SIZE	CAL.	FAT Total (g)	FAT As % of Cal.	SAT. FAT Total (g)	SAT. FAT As % of Cal.	CHOL. (mg)
Fruit & Fibre—Dates, Raisins, Walnuts, Post, 1 cup (60 g)	210	3	13	<1	2	0
Fruity Pebbles, Post, ¾ cup (27 g)	110	1	8	<1	4	0
Golden Grahams, General Mills, ¾ cup (30 g)	120	1	8	0	0	0
Granola Bars, Lowfat, Kellogg's, (Crunchy Apple Spice) 1 bar (21 g)	80	<2	17	0	0	0
Granola, Hearty, C.W. Post, 1 oz.	128	4	28	3	21	0
Granola, Nature Valley, ⅓ cup (1 oz.)	125	5	36	3	22	tr
Granola with Almonds, Sun Country, 1 oz.	130	5	35	1	7	0
Granola with Raisins, Hearty, C.W. Post, 1 oz.	125	4	29	3	32	0
Granola with Raisins, Sun Country, 1 oz.	125	5	36	1	7	0
Grape-Nuts, Post, ½ cup (58 g)	200	0	0	0	0	0
Grape-Nuts Flakes, Post, ¾ cup (29 g)	100	1	9	0	0	0
Honeycomb, Post, 1⅓ cups (29 g)	110	0	0	0	0	0
Just Right with Fiber Nuggets, Kellogg's, 1 cup (55 g)	210	<2	9	0	<1	0
Just Right with Fruit & Nuts, Kellogg's, 1 cup (55 g)	200	2	9	0	0	0
Kix, General Mills, 1⅓ cups (30 g)	120	1	8	0	0	0
Life, Quaker Oats, ¾ cup (32 g)	120	<2	11	0	0	0
Life, Cinnamon, Quaker Oats, 1 cup (50 g)	190	2	9	0	0	0

FOOD/PORTION SIZE	CAL.	FAT Total (g)	FAT As % of Cal.	SAT. FAT Total (g)	SAT. FAT As % of Cal.	CHOL (mg)
Lucky Charms, General Mills, 1 cup (30 g)	120	1	8	0	0	0
Müeslix Crispy Blend, Kellogg's, ⅔ cup (55 g)	200	3	14	0	0	0
Multi-Grain Squares, Kellogg's, Healthy Choice, 1¼ cups (55 g)	190	1	5	0	0	0
Natural Bran Flakes, Post, ⅔ cup (28 g)	90	0	0	0	0	0
Nutri-Grain Almonds & Raisins, Kellogg's, 1¼ cups (55 g)	200	3	14	0	0	0
Nutri-Grain Wheat & Raisins, Kellogg's, 1¼ cups (55 g)	170	1	5	0	0	0
Oat Bran, Quaker, 1¼ cups (57 g)	210	3	13	<1	2	0
Product 19, Kellogg's, 1 cup (30 g, 1.1 oz.)	110	0	0	0	0	0
Puffed Rice, Quaker Oats, ½ oz.	54	tr	na	tr	na	0
Puffed Wheat, Quaker Oats, 1¼ cups (15 g)	50	0	0	0	0	0
Raisin Bran, Kellogg's, 1 cup (55 g, 2 oz.)	170	1	5	0	0	0
Raisin Bran, Post, 1 cup (59 g)	190	1	5	0	0	0
Rice Chex, Ralston Purina, 1 cup (31 g)	120	0	0	0	0	0
Rice Krispies, Kellogg's, 1¼ cups (30 g, 1.1 oz.)	110	0	0	0	0	0
Shredded Wheat, Nabisco, 2 biscuits (46 g)	160	<1	3	0	0	0
Shredded Wheat, Spoon Size, Nabisco, 1 cup (49 g)	170	<1	3	0	0	0
Smurf-Berry Crunch, 1 oz.	110	1	8	tr	na	0
Special K, Kellogg's, 1 cup (30 g, 1.1 oz.)	110	0	0	0	0	0

BREADS & CEREALS

FOOD/PORTION SIZE	CAL.	FAT Total (g)	FAT As % of Cal.	SAT. FAT Total (g)	SAT. FAT As % of Cal.	CHOL. (mg)
Sugar Frosted Flakes, Kellogg's, ¾ cup (30 g, 1.1 oz.)	120	0	0	0	0	0
Super Golden Crisp, Post, ¾ cup (27 g)	110	0	0	0	0	0
Trix, General Mills, 1 cup (30 g)	120	<2	11	0	0	0
Wheat Chex, Ralston Purina, ¾ cup (50 g)	190	1	5	0	0	0
Wheat Germ, Honey Crunch, Kretschmer, 2 tbsp. (13 g)	50	1	18	0	0	0
Wheaties, General Mills, 1 cup (30 g)	110	1	8	0	0	0
CEREALS, HOT						
Corn grits, regular/quick, enriched, 1 cup	145	tr	na	tr	na	0
Cream of Wheat, Instant, Nabisco, 1 packet (28 g)	100	0	0	0	0	0
Cream of Wheat, Mix 'n Eat, plain, 1 packet	100	tr	na	0	0	0
Cream of Wheat, Original, instant, 1 packet (28 g)	100	0	0	0	0	0
Oat Bran, Quaker Oats, ½ cup (40 g)	150	3	18	1	6	0
Oats, Instant, Apple Cinnamon, Quaker Oats, 1 packet (35 g)	130	<2	10	<1	3	0
Oats, Instant, Bananas & Cream, Quaker Oats, 1 packet (35 g)	140	<3	16	<1	3	0
Oats, Instant, Blueberries & Cream, Quaker Oats, 1 packet (35 g)	130	<3	17	<1	3	0
Oats, Instant, Cinnamon Spice, Quaker Oats, 1 packet (46 g)	170	2	11	0	0	0

FOOD/PORTION SIZE	CAL.	FAT Total (g)	FAT As % of Cal.	SAT. FAT Total (g)	SAT. FAT As % of Cal.	CHOL. (mg)
Oats, Instant, Maple & Brown Sugar, Quaker Oats, 1 packet (43 g)	160	2	11	<1	3	0
Oats, Instant, Peaches & Cream, Quaker Oats, 1 packet (35 g)	130	2	14	<1	3	0
Oats, Instant, Raisin Date Walnut, Quaker Oats, 1 packet (37 g)	130	<3	17	<1	3	0
Oats, Instant, Regular, Quaker Oats, dry, 1 packet (28 g)	100	2	18	0	0	0
Oats, Instant, Strawberries & Cream, Quaker Oats, 1 packet (35 g)	130	2	14	<1	<3	0
Oats, Old Fashioned, Quaker Oats, ½ cup cooked (40 g dry)	150	3	18	<1	3	0

CRACKERS

FOOD/PORTION SIZE	CAL.	FAT Total (g)	FAT As % of Cal.	SAT. FAT Total (g)	SAT. FAT As % of Cal.	CHOL. (mg)
Cheese, plain, 1-in. square, 10 crackers	50	3	54	<1	16	6
Cheese, sandwich/peanut butter, 1 sandwich	40	2	45	<1	9	1
Graham, Honey, Honey Maid, Nabisco, 4 crackers (28 g)	120	3	23	<1	4	0
Graham, plain, 2½-in. square, 2 crackers	60	1	15	<1	6	0
Ritz, Nabisco, 5 crackers (16 g)	80	4	45	<1	6	0
Rye wafers, whole-grain, 2 wafers	55	1	16	<1	5	0
Rykrisp, (Natural), 2 crackers (16 g)	70	<2	19	0	0	0
Saltines, 4 crackers	50	1	18	<1	9	4
Snack-type, standard, 1 round cracker	15	1	60	<1	12	0

BREADS & CEREALS

FOOD/PORTION SIZE	CAL.	FAT Total (g)	FAT As % of Cal.	SAT. FAT Total (g)	SAT. FAT As % of Cal.	CHOL. (mg)
Town House, Low Sodium, Keebler, 5 crackers (16 g)	80	<5	51	1	11	0
Wheat, thin, 4 crackers	35	1	26	<1	13	0
Wheatables, 50% Reduced Fat, Keebler, 29 crackers (30 g)	130	<4	24	1	7	0
Wheat Thins, Original, Nabisco, 16 crackers (29 g)	140	6	39	1	6	0
Whole Wheat Wafers, Triscuit, Nabisco, 7 wafers	140	5	32	1	6	0
MUFFINS						
Apple Streusel, Breakfast, Hostess, 1 muffin	100	1	9	tr	na	0
Banana Nut, Frozen, Healthy Choice, 1 muffin	180	6	30	tr	na	0
Blueberry, Bakery Style Muffin Mix, Duncan Hines, about ¼ cup mix (30 g)	100	<3	23	<1	5	0
Blueberry, Frozen, Healthy Choice, 1 muffin	190	4	19	tr	na	0
Blueberry, mix, 1 muffin	140	5	32	1	6	45
Blueberry, Wild, Betty Crocker, regular recipe, 1 muffin (40 g mix)	140	<2	10	<1	3	0
Same as above, no-cholesterol recipe	70	tr	na	na	na	0
Bran, mix, 1 muffin	140	4	26	1	6	28
Bran, with Raisins, Pepperidge Farm, 1 muffin (58 g)	150	<3	15	<1	3	0
English, Bay's, 1 muffin (57 g)	140	<2	10	<1	3	0
English, plain, enriched, 1 muffin	140	1	6	<1	2	0
English, Thomas', 1 muffin (57 g)	120	1	8	0	0	0

FOOD/PORTION SIZE	CAL.	FAT Total (g)	FAT As % of Cal.	SAT. FAT Total (g)	SAT. FAT As % of Cal.	CHOL (mg)
ROLLS						
Dinner, enriched commercial, 1 roll	85	2	21	<1	5	tr
Dinner Rolls, Crescent, Pillsbury, 2 rolls (57 g)	200	11	50	<3	11	0
Frankfurter/hamburger, enriched commercial, 1 roll	115	2	16	<1	4	tr
Hard, enriched commercial, 1 roll	155	2	12	<1	2	tr
Hoagie/submarine, enriched commercial, 1 roll	400	8	18	2	5	tr
MISCELLANEOUS						
Bagel, plain/water, enriched, 1 bagel	200	2	9	<1	1	0
Bagels, Cinnamon Raisin, Lender's, 1 bagel (71 g, 2.5 oz.)	200	<2	7	0	0	0
Bagels, Egg, Lender's, 1 bagel (76 g)	200	1	5	0	0	0
Bagels, Plain, Lender's, 1 bagel (57 g, 2 oz.)	160	1	6	0	0	0
Bran, unprocessed, Quaker Oats, ½ oz.	21	tr	na	tr	na	0
Breadsticks, Pillsbury, 1 stick (39 g)	110	<3	20	<1	4	0
Croissant, with enriched flour, 1 croissant	235	12	46	4	15	13
Melba toast, plain, 1 piece	20	tr	na	<1	5	0
Pancakes & Waffle Mix, Original, Aunt Jemima, 4 4-in. pancakes (110 g)	230	6	23	<2	6	70
Stuffing, Herb Seasoned, Pepperidge Farm, ¾ cup (43 g)	170	<2	8	0	0	0

BREADS & CEREALS

FOOD/PORTION SIZE	CAL.	FAT Total (g)	FAT As % of Cal.	SAT. FAT Total (g)	SAT. FAT As % of Cal.	CHOL. (mg)
Stuffing Mix, Chicken Flavored, Stove Top One Step, about ½ cup mix (28 g)	120	3	23	<1	4	0
Stuffing Mix, Croutettes, Kellogg's, approx. 1 cup (35 g)	120	0	0	0	0	0
Stuffing mix, moist, prepared from mix, 1 cup	420	26	56	5	11	67
Taco Shell, Ortega, 2 shells (30 g)	140	7	45	1	6	0
Tortilla, corn, 1 tortilla	65	1	14	<1	1	0
Tortilla, Corn, Azteca, 2 tortillas (34 g)	90	1	10	0	0	0
Tortillas, Flour, 7-inch, Azteca, 1 tortilla (33 g)	90	2	20	0	0	0
Waffles, Kellogg's Special K, Eggo, 2 waffles (58 g)	140	0	0	0	0	0
Wheat Bran, Toasted, Kretschmer, ¼ cup (16 g)	30	1	30	0	0	0

Candy

FOOD/PORTION SIZE	CAL.	FAT Total (g)	FAT As % of Cal.	SAT. FAT Total (g)	SAT. FAT As % of Cal.	CHOL. (mg)
Almond Joy, Snack Size, 2 bars (39 g)	200	11	50	8	36	0
Baby Ruth, 1 bar (2.1 oz.)	290	14	43	8	25	0
Butterfinger Bar, ⅓ bar (36 g)	170	7	37	4	19	0
Butter Mints, Kraft, 1 mint	8	0	0	0	0	0
Caramels, Kraft, 5 caramels (41 g)	170	3	16	1	5	5
Chocolate Fudgies, Kraft, 1 fudgie	35	1	26	0	0	0

FOOD/PORTION SIZE	CAL.	FAT		SAT. FAT		CHOL. (mg)
		Total (g)	As % of Cal.	Total (g)	As % of Cal.	
Chocolate, sweet dark, 1 oz.	152	10	59	6	36	0
Crunch, Nestlé, 1 bar (44 g)	230	12	47	7	27	5
Fudge, chocolate, plain, 1 oz.	117	3	23	2	15	1
Gum drops, 1 oz.	100	tr	na	tr	na	0
Hard candy, 1 oz.	110	0	0	0	0	0
Jelly beans, 1 oz.	105	tr	na	tr	na	0
Jet-Puffed Marshmallows, Kraft, 5 marshmallows (34 g)	110	0	0	0	0	0
Kisses, Hershey's, 8 pieces (39 g)	210	12	51	8	34	10
Kit-Kat, 1 bar	220	12	49	8	33	5
M & M's Peanut Chocolate Candies, 1.5 oz., ¼ cup (42 g)	220	11	45	4	16	5
M & M's Plain Chocolate Candies, ¼ cup (42 g)	200	9	41	5	23	5
Marshmallows, 1 oz.	91	0	0	0	0	0
Milk chocolate, plain, 1 oz.	147	9	55	5	31	6
Milk chocolate, with almonds, 1 oz.	152	9	53	5	30	5
Milk chocolate, with peanuts, 1 oz.	154	10	58	4	23	5
Milk chocolate, with rice cereal, 1 oz.	140	7	45	4	26	6
Milky Way Bar, 1 bar (61 g)	280	11	35	5	16	5
Mr. Goodbar, Hershey's, 1.75 oz.	280	18	58	7	23	5
Party Mints, Kraft, 7 pieces (15 g)	60	0	0	0	0	0
Peanut Brittle, Kraft, 5 pieces (170 g)	170	5	26	1	5	0
Peanut Butter Cups, Reese's, 2 pieces (34 g)	190	11	52	4	19	<5
Snickers, Minis, 4 pieces (36 g)	170	8	42	3	16	5
Special Dark, Hershey's, 1 bar	220	12	49	7	29	3

CONSUMER GUIDE®   59

Cheese

FOOD/PORTION SIZE	CAL.	FAT Total (g)	FAT As % of Cal.	SAT. FAT Total (g)	SAT. FAT As % of Cal.	CHOL. (mg)
American Flavored, Singles Pasteurized Process Cheese Product, Light n' Lively, 1 oz.	70	4	51	3	39	13
American Flavor, Imitation Pasteurized Process Cheese Food, Golden Image, 1 oz.	90	6	60	2	20	5
American Flavor Process Cheese, Low Sodium, Weight Watchers, 1 slice (21 g)	50	2	36	1	18	5
American, Pasteurized Process Cheese Slices, Deluxe, Kraft, 1 slice (19 g)	70	6	77	4	51	15
American Process Cheese, Borden Lite-line, 1 oz.	50	2	36	1	18	13
American, Sharp, Pasteurized Process Slices, Old English, Kraft, 1 slice (28 g)	110	9	74	5	49	30
American Singles Pasteurized Process Cheese Food, Kraft, 1 slice (19 g)	60	5	75	3	45	15
Blue, 1 oz.	100	8	72	6	54	21
Blue, Natural Crumbles, Kraft, 1 oz. (28 g)	100	8	72	6	54	30
Brick, Natural, Kraft, 1 oz.(28 g)	110	9	74	6	50	30
Camembert, 1 wedge (1/3 of 4-oz. container)	115	9	70	6	47	27
Cheddar, Extra Sharp, Cold Pack Cheese Food, Cracker Barrel, 1 oz. (28 g)	110	9	74	6	49	30
Cheddar, Free 'n Lean, Alpine Lace, 1/6 bar (28 g)	45	0	0	0	0	5

FOOD/PORTION SIZE	CAL.	FAT Total (g)	FAT As % of Cal.	SAT. FAT Total (g)	SAT. FAT As % of Cal.	CHOL. (mg)
Cheddar, Natural, Kraft, 1 oz. (28 g)	110	9	74	6	49	30
Cheddar, Port Wine, Cheese Log with Almonds, Cracker Barrel, 1 oz.	90	6	60	3	30	15
Cheddar, Port Wine, Cold Pack Cheese Food, Cracker Barrel, 1 oz.	100	7	63	4	36	20
Cheddar, Sharp, Cheese Ball with Almonds, Cracker Barrel, 1 oz.	100	7	63	3	27	20
Cheddar, Sharp, Cold Pack Cheese Food, Cracker Barrel, 1 oz. (28 g)	110	9	74	6	49	30
Cheddar, Sharp, Process Cheese, Borden Lite-line, 1 oz.	50	2	36	1	18	15
Cheddar, Sharp, Reduced Fat Natural, Kraft, 1 oz. (28 g)	80	5	56	<4	39	20
Cheddar, shredded, 1 cup	455	34	67	23	45	120
Cheddar, Smokey, Cheese Log with Almonds, Cracker Barrel, 1 oz.	90	6	60	3	30	15
Cheese Food, Cold Pack with Real Bacon, Cracker Barrel, 1 oz.	90	7	70	4	40	20
Cheese Food, Pasteurized Process Sharp Singles, Kraft Free, 1 slice (21 g)	30	0	0	0	0	5
Cheese Spread, Mild Mexican, Velveeta, 1 oz. (28 g)	80	6	68	4	45	20
Cheese Spread, Pasteurized Process, Velveeta, 1 oz. (28 g)	80	6	68	4	45	20
Cheese Spread, Slices, Pasteurized Process, Velveeta, 1 slice (21 g)	60	4	60	3	45	15

CHEESE

FOOD/PORTION SIZE	CAL.	FAT Total (g)	FAT As % of Cal.	SAT. FAT Total (g)	SAT. FAT As % of Cal.	CHOL. (mg)
Cheez Whiz, Mild Salsa, Pasteurized Process Cheese Spread, 2 tbsp. (33 g)	90	7	70	5	50	25
Cheez Whiz, Pasteurized Process Cheese Spread, 2 tbsp. (33 g)	90	7	70	5	50	20
Cheez Whiz, with Jalapeño Pepper, Pasteurized Process Cheese Spread, 2 tbsp. (33 g)	90	8	80	5	50	25
Cottage, creamed, large curd, 1 cup	235	10	38	6	23	34
Cottage, creamed, small curd, 1 cup	215	9	35	6	25	31
Cottage, Lite n' Lively, ½ cup (115 g)	80	<2	17	1	11	15
Cottage, low-fat (2%), 1 cup	205	4	18	3	13	19
Cottage, uncreamed, dry curd, 1 cup	125	1	7	<1	3	10
Cream Cheese, Fat Free, Philadelphia Brand, 1 oz. (28 g)	25	0	0	0	0	<5
Cream Cheese, Philadelphia Brand, 1 oz. (28 g)	100	10	90	6	54	30
Cream Cheese Product, Pasteurized Process, Light, Philadelphia Brand, 1 oz. (28 g)	70	6	77	4	51	20
Cream Cheese, Whipped, with Chives & Onions, Philadelphia Brand, 3 tbsp. (31 g)	100	9	81	6	54	30
Cream Cheese, Whipped, with Smoked Salmon, Philadelphia Brand, 2 tbsp. (31 g)	100	9	81	6	54	30

FOOD/PORTION SIZE	CAL.	FAT		SAT. FAT		CHOL. (mg)
		Total (g)	As % of Cal.	Total (g)	As % of Cal.	
Cream Cheese with Chives, Philadelphia Brand, 3 tbsp. (31 g)	100	9	81	6	54	30
Cream Cheese with Chives & Onion, Soft, Philadelphia Brand, 2 tbsp. (31 g)	110	10	81	7	57	30
Cream Cheese with Olive & Pimento, Soft, Philadelphia Brand, 2 tbsp. (31 g)	100	9	81	6	54	30
Cream Cheese with Pineapple, Soft, Philadelphia Brand, 2 tbsp. (32 g)	100	9	81	6	54	30
Cream Cheese with Smoked Salmon, Soft, Philadelphia Brand, 2 tbsp. (31 g)	100	9	81	6	54	30
Cream Cheese with Strawberries, Soft, Philadelphia Brand, 2 tbsp. (32 g)	100	9	81	6	54	30
Feta, 1 oz.	75	6	72	4	48	25
Gouda, Natural, Kraft, 1 oz.	110	9	74	5	41	30
Jalapeño Pasteurized Process Cheese Spread, Kraft, 1 oz.	80	6	68	4	45	20
Jalapeño Singles Pasteurized Process Cheese Food, Kraft, 1 oz. (28 g)	90	7	70	5	50	20
Limburger Pasteurized Process Cheese Spread, Mohawk Valley, 2 tbsp. (32 g)	80	7	79	<5	51	20
Monterey Jack, Natural, Shredded, Sargento, ¼ cup (28 g)	100	9	81	5	45	30

CHEESE

FOOD/PORTION SIZE	CAL.	FAT Total (g)	FAT As % of Cal.	SAT. FAT Total (g)	SAT. FAT As % of Cal.	CHOL. (mg)
Monterey, Singles, Pasteurized Process Cheese Food, Kraft, ¾ oz. (21 g)	70	5	64	<4	45	15
Mozzarella, made with part-skim milk, 1 oz.	72	5	63	3	38	16
Mozzarella, made with whole milk, 1 oz.	80	6	68	4	45	22
Mozzarella, Part-Skim, Low Moisture, Kraft, 1 oz. (28 g)	80	5	56	4	45	20
Mozzarella, Preferred Light, Shredded, Sargento, ¼ cup (28 g)	60	3	45	2	30	10
Mozzarella, Truly Lite, Frigo, 1 oz. (28 g)	60	<3	38	<2	23	15
Muenster, 1 oz.	104	8	69	4	35	27
Neufchâtel, ⅓ Less Fat, Philadelphia Brand, 1 oz. (28 g)	70	6	77	4	51	20
Parmesan, grated, 1 tbsp.	25	2	72	1	36	4
Parmesan, Grated, Kraft, 1 tbsp. (5 g)	20	<2	68	1	45	5
Parmesan, Natural, Kraft, 1 oz.	100	7	63	4	36	20
Parmesan, Preferred Light Grated Gourmet, Sargento, 1 tbsp.	25	2	72	tr	na	4
Pimento Singles Pasteurized Process Cheese Food, Kraft, ¾ oz. (21 g)	70	5	64	<4	45	15
Pimento Spread, Kraft, 2 tbsp. (32 g)	80	6	68	4	45	20
Provolone, 1 oz.	100	8	72	5	45	20
Ricotta, made with part-skim milk, 1 cup	340	19	50	12	32	76
Ricotta, made with whole milk, 1 cup	430	30	63	20	42	126

CREAM & CREAMERS

FOOD/PORTION SIZE	CAL.	FAT Total (g)	FAT As % of Cal.	SAT. FAT Total (g)	SAT. FAT As % of Cal.	CHOL. (mg)
Ricotta, Natural Nonfat, Polly-O Free, 1 oz.	25	0	0	0	0	0
Ricotta, Reduced Fat, Polly-O Lite, 1 oz.	35	2	51	1	26	5
Romano, Grated, Kraft, 1 tbsp. (5 g)	25	<2	54	1	36	5
Romano, Natural, Casino, 1 oz.	100	7	63	4	36	20
Swiss, 1 oz.	105	8	69	5	43	26
Swiss Flavor Process Cheese, Fat Free, Borden, 1 slice (21 g)	30	0	0	0	0	0
Swiss, Natural, Kraft, 1 slice (23 g)	90	6	60	4	40	20
Swiss, Preferred Light, Sargento, 1 slice (28 g)	80	4	45	2	23	15
Swiss Singles Pasteurized Process Cheese Food, Kraft, 1 slice (21 g)	70	5	64	3	39	15

Cream & Creamers

FOOD/PORTION SIZE	CAL.	FAT Total (g)	FAT As % of Cal.	SAT. FAT Total (g)	SAT. FAT As % of Cal.	CHOL. (mg)
Coffee Rich, ½ oz.	20	2	90	tr	na	0
Cool Whip Extra Creamy Dairy Recipe Whipped Topping, Birds Eye, 2 tbsp. (9 g)	30	2	60	2	60	0
Cool Whip Lite Whipped Topping, Birds Eye, 1 tbsp.	8	tr	na	na	na	0
Cool Whip Non-Dairy Whipped Topping, Birds Eye, 2 tbsp. (8 g)	25	<2	54	<2	54	0

CREAM & CREAMERS

FOOD/PORTION SIZE	CAL.	FAT Total (g)	FAT As % of Cal.	SAT. FAT Total (g)	SAT. FAT As % of Cal.	CHOL. (mg)
Cream, sweet, half-and-half, 1 tbsp.	20	2	90	2	90	6
Cream, sweet, light/ coffee/table, 1 tbsp.	30	3	90	2	60	10
Cream, sweet, whipping, unwhipped, heavy, 1 cup	820	88	97	55	60	326
Cream, sweet, whipping, unwhipped, heavy, 1 tbsp.	50	6	100	4	72	21
Cream, sweet, whipping, unwhipped, light, 1 cup	700	69	89	46	59	272
Cream, sweet, whipping, unwhipped, light, 1 tbsp.	44	5	100	3	61	17
Cream, whipped topping, pressurized, 1 tbsp.	10	1	90	<1	72	0
Creamer, sweet, imitation, liquid, 1 tbsp.	20	1	45	<2	63	0
Cream Topping, Real, Kraft, 2 tbsp. (7 g)	20	<2	68	1	45	5
Sour Cream, Fat Free, Breakstone's Free, 2 tbsp. (32 g)	35	0	0	0	0	<5
Sour Cream, Land O Lakes, 1 tbsp.	20	1	45	1	45	1
Sour Cream, Light, Sealtest Light, 2 tbsp. (31 g)	40	<3	56	2	45	10
Whipped Topping, Kraft, 2 tbsp. (7 g)	20	<2	68	1	45	0
Whipped topping, sweet, imitation, frozen, 1 tbsp.	15	1	60	1	60	0
Whipped topping, sweet, imitation, pressurized, 1 tbsp.	10	1	90	<1	72	2
Whipped Topping Mix, Dream Whip, prepared with water, 2 tbsp.	10	0	0	0	0	0
Whipped Topping Mix, Reduced Calorie, D-Zerta, prepared, 1 tbsp.	8	1	100	tr	na	0

Eggs

FOOD/PORTION SIZE	CAL.	FAT Total (g)	FAT As % of Cal.	SAT. FAT Total (g)	SAT. FAT As % of Cal.	CHOL. (mg)
Egg Beaters, Fleischmann's, ¼ cup (61 g)	30	0	0	0	0	0
Egg Substitute, Scramblers, ¼ cup (57 g)	35	0	0	0	0	0
Large, fried in butter, 1 egg	83	7	76	3	33	278
Large, hard-cooked, 1 egg	80	6	68	2	23	213
Large, poached, 1 egg	80	6	68	2	23	213
Large, raw, white only, 1 white	15	0	0	0	0	0
Large, raw, whole, 1 egg	80	6	68	2	23	213
Large, raw, yolk only, 1 yolk	65	6	83	2	28	213
Scrambled, with milk, cooked in margarine, 1 egg	100	7	63	2	18	215

Fast Foods

FOOD/PORTION SIZE	CAL.	FAT Total (g)	FAT As % of Cal.	SAT. FAT Total (g)	SAT. FAT As % of Cal.	CHOL. (mg)
ARBY'S						
Beef N' Cheddar Sandwich	508	27	47	8	14	52
Chicken Breast Fillet Sandwich	445	23	46	3	6	45
Dressing, Blue Cheese, 2 oz.	295	31	95	6	18	50
Dressing, Honey French, 2 oz.	322	27	75	4	11	0
French Dip Sandwich	368	15	37	6	15	43
French Fries	246	13	48	3	11	0
Italian Sub	671	40	54	13	17	69
Light Roast Beef Deluxe Sandwich	294	10	31	4	11	42
Light Roast Chicken Deluxe Sandwich	276	7	23	2	6	33

FAST FOODS

FOOD/PORTION SIZE	CAL.	FAT Total (g)	FAT As % of Cal.	SAT. FAT Total (g)	SAT. FAT As % of Cal.	CHOL. (mg)
Light Roast Turkey Deluxe Sandwich	260	6	17	2	7	33
Salad, Chef	205	10	42	4	17	126
Salad, Garden	117	5	40	3	21	12
Salad, Roast Chicken	204	7	32	3	15	43
Salad, Side	25	<1	10	tr	na	0
Turkey Sub	486	19	43	5	12	51
BURGER KING						
Bacon Double Cheeseburger	470	28	54	13	25	100
Cheeseburger	300	14	42	6	18	45
Chicken BK Broiler Sandwich	280	10	32	2	6	50
Chunky Chicken Salad	142	4	25	1	6	49
Croissan'wich with Bacon	353	23	59	8	20	230
Croissan'wich with Ham	351	22	56	7	18	236
Croissan'wich with Sausage	534	40	67	14	24	258
French Fries, lightly salted, medium	372	20	48	5	12	0
French Toast Sticks, 1 order	440	27	55	7	14	0
Hamburger	260	10	35	4	14	30
Ocean Catch Fish Fillet	450	28	56	7	14	30
Onion Rings, 1 order	339	19	50	5	13	0
Pie, Apple	320	14	39	4	11	0
Salad, Chef	178	9	46	4	20	103
Whopper	570	31	49	10	16	80
Whopper with Cheese	660	38	52	15	20	105
DAIRY QUEEN						
Banana Split	510	11	19	8	14	30
Fish Fillet Sandwich	370	16	39	3	7	45
Fish Fillet Sandwich with Cheese	420	21	45	6	13	60
Grilled Chicken Fillet Sandwich	300	8	24	2	6	50

FOOD/PORTION SIZE	CAL.	FAT Total (g)	FAT As % of Cal.	SAT. FAT Total (g)	SAT. FAT As % of Cal.	CHOL. (mg)
Hamburger, Single	310	13	38	6	17	45
Heath Blizzard, Small	560	23	37	11	18	40
Hot Dog	280	16	51	6	19	25
Hot Dog w/Chili	320	19	53	7	20	30
Malt, Regular Vanilla	610	14	21	8	12	45
Parfait, Peanut Buster	710	32	41	10	13	30
Shake, Regular Chocolate	540	14	23	8	13	45
Sundae, Regular Chocolate	300	7	21	5	15	20
DOMINO'S						
Pizza, Cheese, Deep Dish, 2 slices	560	24	39	9	14	32
Pizza, Cheese, Thin Crust, 2 slices	364	16	40	6	15	26
Pizza, Extra Cheese & Pepperoni, Deep Dish, 2 slices	671	33	44	13	17	54
Pizza, Ham, Hand-Tossed, 2 slices	362	10	25	5	12	26
Pizza, Ham, Thin Crust, 2 slices	388	17	39	7	16	35
Pizza, Italian Sausage & Mushroom, 2 slices	442	21	43	9	18	41
Pizza, Veggie, Deep Dish, 2 slices	576	25	39	9	14	32
DUNKIN' DONUTS						
Apple Filled Cinnamon	250	11	40	<3	8	0
Boston Kreme	240	11	41	<3	9	0
Chocolate Frosted Yeast Ring	200	10	45	<2	9	0
Glazed Cruller	260	11	38	<3	8	0
Glazed Yeast Ring	200	9	41	2	9	0
Jelly Filled	220	9	37	<2	7	0
Plain Cake Ring	262	18	62	<4	13	0
Powdered Cake Ring	270	16	53	<4	11	0

FAST FOODS

FOOD/PORTION SIZE	CAL.	FAT Total (g)	FAT As % of Cal.	SAT. FAT Total (g)	SAT. FAT As % of Cal.	CHOL. (mg)
KENTUCKY FRIED CHICKEN						
Biscuit, 2 oz.	200	12	54	3	14	2
Coleslaw, 3.2 oz.	114	6	47	1	8	<5
Extra Tasty Crispy, breast, 5.9 oz.	470	28	54	7	13	80
Extra Tasty Crispy, drumstick, 2.4 oz.	190	11	52	3	14	60
Extra Tasty Crispy, wing, 1.9 oz.	240	13	49	4	15	45
Hot & Spicy, breast, 6.5 oz.	530	35	59	8	14	110
Hot & Spicy, drumstick, 2.3 oz.	190	11	52	3	14	50
Hot Wings, six wings, 4.8 oz.	471	33	63	8	15	150
Kentucky Nuggets, six, 3.4 oz.	284	18	57	4	13	66
Mashed Potatoes with Gravy, 4.2 oz.	109	5	41	<1	na	<1
Quarter, breast & wing, Rotisserie Gold, 6.2 oz.	335	19	50	<6	15	157
Quarter, breast & wing, Rotisserie Gold, w/o skin or wing, 4.1 oz.	199	6	27	<2	8	97
LONG JOHN SILVER'S						
Baked Chicken, Light Herb	120	4	30	<2	9	65
Baked Fish, Lemon Crumb, 3 pieces	150	1	6	<1	<4	110
Baked Fish, Lemon Crumb, 3 pieces, Rice, and Small Salad (w/o dressing)	610	13	19	<3	3	125
Chicken Plank, 1 piece, 2 oz.	120	6	45	<2	12	15
Clams, 2 hushpuppies, fries, and slaw, 12.7 oz.	990	52	47	11	10	75
Seafood Gumbo, with cod, 7 oz.	120	8	60	<3	16	25

FOOD/PORTION SIZE	CAL.	FAT Total (g)	FAT As % of Cal.	SAT. FAT Total (g)	SAT. FAT As % of Cal.	CHOL. (mg)
McDONALD'S						
Big Mac	490	27	50	9	17	90
Biscuit with Bacon, Egg, and Cheese	440	26	53	8	16	240
Biscuit with Sausage	420	28	60	8	17	45
Biscuit with Sausage and Egg	520	34	59	11	19	270
Cheeseburger	300	13	39	5	15	50
Chicken McNuggets (6 pieces)	270	15	50	<4	12	55
Cone, Lowfat Frozen Yogurt, Vanilla	110	1	8	<1	4	5
Cookies, Chocolaty Chip, 2 oz.	330	15	41	4	11	5
Cookies, McDonaldland, 2 oz.	290	9	28	1	3	0
Danish, Apple	360	16	40	5	13	40
Danish, Cinnamon Raisin	430	22	46	7	15	50
Danish, Raspberry	390	16	37	5	12	45
Dressing, Lite Vinaigrette, 2 oz.	50	2	36	0	0	0
Dressing, Ranch, 2 oz.	230	21	82	3	12	23
Egg McMuffin	280	11	35	4	13	235
Eggs, Scrambled, 2 eggs	140	10	64	3	19	425
Filet-O-Fish sandwich	370	18	44	4	10	50
French Fries, small	220	12	49	<3	10	0
Hamburger	250	9	32	<4	13	40
Hashbrowns	130	7	48	1	7	0
Hotcakes with 2 pats margarine and syrup	410	9	20	<2	3	10
McLean Deluxe	320	10	28	4	11	60
Pie, Apple	280	15	48	2	6	0
Quarter Pounder	400	20	44	8	18	85
Quarter Pounder with Cheese	490	27	50	10	18	115
Salad, Chef	170	9	48	4	21	110

FAST FOODS

FOOD/PORTION SIZE	CAL.	FAT Total (g)	FAT As % of Cal.	SAT. FAT Total (g)	SAT. FAT As % of Cal.	CHOL. (mg)
Salad, Chicken, Chunky	150	4	24	1	6	80
Salad, Garden	50	2	36	<1	9	65
Sauce, Barbecue, 1 serving	50	0	0	0	0	0
Sauce, Hot Mustard, 1 serving	70	<4	45	<1	6	5
Sauce, Sweet-n-Sour, 1 serving	60	0	0	0	0	0
Sausage	160	15	84	5	28	45
Sausage McMuffin	350	20	51	7	18	60
Sausage McMuffin with Egg	430	25	52	8	17	270
Shake, Chocolate	350	6	15	4	10	25
Shake, Strawberry	340	5	13	3	8	25
Shake, Vanilla	310	5	15	3	9	25
Sundae, Hot Caramel Lowfat Frozen Yogurt	270	3	10	<2	5	15
Sundae, Hot Fudge Lowfat Frozen Yogurt	240	3	11	2	8	5
Sundae, Strawberry Lowfat Frozen Yogurt	210	1	4	<1	2	5
PIZZA HUT						
Pizza, Bigfoot Cheese, 1 slice medium	179	5	25	3	15	14
Pizza, Hand-Tossed, Cheese, 1 slice medium (15-inch)	253	9	32	4	14	25
Pizza, Hand-Tossed, Supreme, 1 slice medium (15-inch)	289	12	37	3	9	29
Pizza, Pan, Super Supreme, 1 slice medium (15-inch)	302	19	57	4	12	32
Pizza, Personal Pan, Pepperoni, whole (5-inch)	675	30	40	10	13	53
Pizza, Personal Pan, Supreme, whole (5-inch)	647	35	49	12	17	53

FOOD/PORTION SIZE	CAL.	FAT		SAT. FAT		CHOL. (mg)
		Total (g)	As % of Cal.	Total (g)	As % of Cal.	
Pizza, Thin 'n Crispy, Pepperoni, 1 slice medium (15-inch)	230	11	43	3	18	27
Pizza, Thin 'n Crispy, Supreme, 1 slice medium (15-inch)	262	14	48	3	10	31
SUBWAY						
BMT Salad	635	52	74	19	27	133
BMT Sub, Italian Roll, 6-inch	491	28	51	10	18	66
Club Salad	173	9	47	3	16	42
Club Sub, Italian Roll, 6-inch	346	11	29	4	10	42
Cold Cut Combo Salad	506	36	64	11	20	165
Cold Cut Combo Sub, Italian Roll, 6-inch	427	20	42	6	13	83
Ham & Cheese Salad	296	18	55	6	18	73
Ham & Cheese Sub, Italian Roll, 6-inch	322	9	25	3	8	36
Meatball Sub, Italian Roll, 6-inch	459	22	43	8	16	44
Roast Beef Salad	340	20	53	7	19	75
Roast Beef Sub, Italian Roll, 6-inch	345	12	31	4	10	38
Seafood & Crab Salad	639	53	75	10	14	56
Seafood & Crab Sub, Italian Roll, 6-inch	493	28	51	5	9	28
Steak & Cheese Sub, Honey Wheat Roll, 6-inch	355	16	41	6	15	41
Tuna Salad	756	68	81	12	14	85
Tuna Sub, Italian Roll, 6-inch	551	36	59	7	11	43
Turkey Breast Salad	297	16	48	5	15	67
Turkey Breast Sub, Italian Roll, 6-inch	322	10	28	3	8	33
Veggies & Cheese Sub, Italian Roll, 6-inch	268	9	30	3	10	10

FAST FOODS

FOOD/PORTION SIZE	CAL.	FAT Total (g)	FAT As % of Cal.	SAT. FAT Total (g)	SAT. FAT As % of Cal.	CHOL. (mg)
TACO BELL (All portions consist of 1 serving)						
Burrito, Bean	391	12	28	4	9	5
Burrito, Beef	432	19	40	8	17	57
Burrito, Chicken	345	13	34	5	13	57
Burrito, Combo	412	16	35	6	13	32
Burrito Supreme	443	19	39	9	18	47
Cinnamon Twists	139	6	39	0	0	0
Meximelt, Beef	262	14	48	7	24	38
Nachos	345	18	47	6	16	9
Nachos Bellgrande	633	34	48	12	17	49
Pintos & Cheese	190	9	43	4	19	14
Pizza, Mexican	574	38	60	12	19	50
Salad, Taco	838	55	59	16	17	79
Salsa	27	0	0	0	0	0
Taco	183	11	54	5	25	32
Taco, Soft	223	11	44	5	20	32
Taco, Soft, Chicken	223	10	40	4	16	58
Taco, Soft, Steak	217	9	37	4	17	31
WENDY'S						
Chicken Club Sandwich	520	25	43	6	10	75
Chicken Nuggets, 6 pieces	280	20	64	5	16	50
Chicken Sandwich, Grilled	290	7	22	<2	5	55
Chili, small, 8 oz.	190	6	28	<3	9	40
Cookie, Chocolate Chip, 1 cookie	280	13	42	4	13	15
Fries, small, 3.2 oz.	240	12	45	<3	9	0
Frosty Dairy Dessert, small	340	10	26	5	11	40
Hamburger, Jr.	270	9	30	3	10	35
Hamburger, Kid's Meal, with White Bun	270	9	30	3	10	35
Hamburger, Single, Plain, ¼ lb	350	15	39	6	15	70
Nuggets Sauce, Barbeque, 1 packet	50	0	0	0	0	0

FOOD/PORTION SIZE	CAL.	FAT Total (g)	FAT As % of Cal.	SAT. FAT Total (g)	SAT. FAT As % of Cal.	CHOL. (mg)
Nuggets Sauce, Honey, 1 packet	45	0	0	0	0	0
Nuggets Sauce, Sweet & Sour, 1 packet	45	0	0	0	0	0
Nuggets Sauce, Sweet Mustard, 1 packet	50	1	18	0	0	0
Potato, Hot Stuffed Baked, Bacon & Cheese	530	18	31	4	7	20
Potato, Hot Stuffed Baked, Broccoli & Cheese	460	14	27	<3	5	0
Potato, Hot Stuffed Baked, Cheese	560	23	37	8	13	30
Potato, Hot Stuffed Baked, Chili & Cheese	610	24	35	9	13	45
Potato, Hot Stuffed Baked, Plain	310	0	0	0	0	0
Potato, Hot Stuffed Baked, Sour Cream & Chives	380	6	15	4	10	15
Salad, Caesar (w/o dressing)	110	5	41	2	16	15
Salad, Deluxe Garden (w/o dressing)	110	6	50	1	8	0
Salad, Taco	580	30	47	11	17	75

Fats & Oils

FOOD/PORTION SIZE	CAL.	FAT Total (g)	FAT As % of Cal.	SAT. FAT Total (g)	SAT. FAT As % of Cal.	CHOL. (mg)
Butter, approx. 1 tbsp.	100	11	99	7	63	31
Butter Buds, Butter Flavored Mix, ½ fl. oz. (1/16 dry oz.)	6	0	0	0	0	0
Butter, Land O Lakes, 1 tbsp. (14 g)	100	11	99	7	63	30
Butter, Whipped, Land O Lakes, 1 tbsp. (9 g)	60	7	100	5	75	20

FATS & OILS

FOOD/PORTION SIZE	CAL.	FAT Total (g)	FAT As % of Cal.	SAT. FAT Total (g)	SAT. FAT As % of Cal.	CHOL. (mg)
Lard, 1 tbsp.	115	13	100	5	39	12
Margarine, Extra Light, Promise, 1 tbsp. (14 g)	50	6	100	1	18	0
Margarine, Fat Free, Promise Ultra, 1 tbsp. (14 g)	5	0	0	0	0	0
Margarine, imitation, soft, 1 tbsp.	50	5	90	1	18	0
Margarine, Light, Parkay, (40% vegetable oil), tub, 1 tbsp. (14 g)	50	6	100	1	18	0
Margarine, Light, Promise Extra, 1 tbsp.	70	7	90	1	13	0
Margarine, Parkay, 1 tbsp. (14 g)	90	10	100	2	20	0
Margarine, regular, hard, 1 tbsp. (⅛ stick)	100	11	99	2	18	0
Margarine, regular, hard, approx. 1 tsp.	35	4	100	1	26	0
Margarine, regular, soft, 1 tbsp.	100	11	99	2	18	0
Margarine, Soft, Parkay, 1 tbsp. (14 g)	60	7	100	<2	23	0
Margarine, Soft, Parkay Corn Oil, 1 tbsp.	100	11	99	2	18	0
Margarine, Soft Diet, Parkay, 1 tbsp. (14 g)	50	6	100	1	18	0
Margarine, spread, hard, approx. 1 tsp.	25	3	100	1	36	0
Margarine, Squeezable, Shedd's Spread Country Crock, 1 tbsp. (14 g)	80	9	100	<2	17	0
Margarine, Squeeze Parkay, 1 tbsp. (14 g)	80	9	100	<2	17	0
Margarine, Stick, Corn Oil, Fleischmann's, 1 tbsp. (14 g)	100	11	99	2	18	0
Margarine, Stick, Sunflower Oil, Promise, 1 tbsp. (14 g)	90	10	100	2	20	0

FOOD/PORTION SIZE	CAL.	FAT Total (g)	FAT As % of Cal.	SAT. FAT Total (g)	SAT. FAT As % of Cal.	CHOL. (mg)
Margarine, Tub, Sunflower Oil, Promise, 1 tbsp. (14 g)	90	10	100	<2	15	0
Oil, Canola, Crisco Puritan, 1 tbsp. (14 g)	120	14	100	1	8	0
Oil, Corn, Mazola, 1 tbsp. (14 g)	120	14	100	2	15	0
Oil, Olive, Bertolli, 1 tbsp. (15 mL)	120	14	100	2	15	0
Oil, peanut, 1 tbsp.	125	14	100	2	14	0
Oil, Safflower, Hollywood, 1 tbsp.	120	14	100	1	8	0
Oil, soybean-cottonseed blend, hydrogenated, 1 tbsp.	125	14	100	3	22	0
Oil, sunflower, 1 tbsp.	125	14	100	1	7	0
Oil, Sunflower, Wesson, 1 tbsp.	120	14	100	<2	11	0
Oil, Vegetable, Crisco, 1 tbsp. (14 g)	120	14	100	<2	11	0
Shortening, Vegetable, Crisco, 1 tbsp. (12 g)	110	12	98	3	25	0
Shortening, Vegetable, Crisco Butter Flavor, 1 tbsp. (12 g)	110	12	98	3	25	0
Spray, Cooking (Vegetable Oil), Pam, 2½-second spray	14	2	100	tr	na	0
Spread, 50% Fat, Parkay, 1 tbsp. (14 g)	60	7	100	<2	23	0
Spread, (70% vegetable oil), I Can't Believe It's Not Butter, 1 tbsp. (14 g)	90	10	100	2	20	0
Spread, Stick, Touch of Butter, (70% oil and dairy spread) Kraft, 1 tbsp. (14 g)	90	10	90	2	20	0
Spread, Tub, (Vegetable), Shedd's, 1 tbsp. (14 g)	60	7	100	<2	23	0

Fish & Shellfish

FOOD/PORTION SIZE	CAL.	FAT Total (g)	FAT As % of Cal.	SAT. FAT Total (g)	SAT. FAT As % of Cal.	CHOL. (mg)
Catfish, breaded, fried, 3 oz.	194	11	52	na	na	69
Catfish, skinless, baked w/o fat, 3 oz.	120	5	38	1	8	60
Clams, Minced, Snow's, ¼ cup (55 g)	25	0	0	0	0	10
Clams, raw, meat only, 3 oz.	65	1	14	<1	4	43
Cod, fillets (frozen), Mrs. Paul's, 1 fillet (120 g) and 1 tsp. relish mix (7 g)	250	11	40	3	11	40
Cod, skinless, broiled w/o fat, 3 oz.	90	1	10	0	0	50
Crabmeat, canned, 1 cup	135	3	20	<1	3	135
Fillets, Crunchy Breaded, Gortons, 2 fillets (108 g)	270	17	57	5	17	25
Fish sticks (frozen), reheated, 4 x ½-in. stick	70	3	39	1	13	26
Flounder, baked, with lemon juice, w/o added fat, 3 oz.	80	1	11	<1	4	59
Haddock, breaded, fried, 3 oz.	175	9	46	2	10	75
Haddock, skinless, baked w/o fat, 3 oz.	90	1	10	0	0	60
Halibut, broiled, with butter, with lemon juice, 3 oz.	140	6	39	3	19	62
Herring, pickled, 3 oz.	190	13	62	4	19	85
Lobster, boiled, 3 oz.	100	1	9	0	0	100
Mackerel, skinless, broiled w/o fat, 3 oz.	190	12	57	3	14	60
Orange roughy, broiled, 3 oz.	130	7	48	0	0	20
Oysters, breaded, fried, 1 oyster	90	5	50	1	10	35
Oysters, raw, meat only, 1 cup	160	4	23	1	6	120
Perch, ocean, breaded, fried, 1 fillet	185	11	54	3	15	66

FOOD/PORTION SIZE	CAL.	FAT Total (g)	FAT As % of Cal.	SAT. FAT Total (g)	SAT. FAT As % of Cal.	CHOL. (mg)
Perch, Ocean, Fillets, Booth, 4 oz.	100	1	9	na	na	na
Pollock, skinless, broiled w/o fat, 3 oz.	100	1	9	0	0	80
Salmon, Pink, (in water) *Bumble Bee,* ½ cup (56 g, drained)	60	2	30	0	0	40
Salmon, Pink (in spring water), *Chicken of the Sea,* 2 oz.	60	2	30	na	na	na
Salmon, red, baked, 3 oz.	140	5	32	1	6	60
Salmon, smoked, 3 oz.	150	8	48	3	18	51
Sardines, canned in oil, drained, 3 oz.	175	11	57	2	10	121
Sardines (in olive oil), *King Oscar,* 3¾ oz.	460	16	31	3	6	na
Scallops, breaded (frozen), reheated, 6 scallops	195	10	46	3	14	70
Scallops, broiled, 3 oz. (5.7 large or 14 small)	150	1	6	0	0	60
Shrimp, boiled, 3 oz.	110	2	16	0	0	160
Shrimp, canned, drained solids, 3 oz.	100	1	9	<1	2	128
Shrimp, French fried, 3 oz. (7 medium)	200	10	45	<3	11	168
Snapper, cooked by dry heat, 3 oz.	109	2	17	na	na	40
Sole, baked, with lemon juice, w/o added fat, 3 oz.	90	1	10	tr	na	49
Surimi seafood, crab flavored, chunk style, ½ cup	84	tr	na	tr	na	25
Trout, Rainbow, skinless, broiled w/o fat, 3 oz.	130	4	28	1	7	60
Tuna, Albacore (in water), *Bumble Bee,* 2 oz. (56 g)	70	1	13	0	0	25

FISH & SHELLFISH

FOOD/PORTION SIZE	CAL.	FAT Total (g)	FAT As % of Cal.	SAT. FAT Total (g)	SAT. FAT As % of Cal.	CHOL. (mg)
Tuna, Chunk Light (in spring water), StarKist, ¼ cup (56 g, drained)	60	<1	8	0	0	30
Tuna, Chunk Light (in vegetable oil), Bumble Bee, about ¼ cup (56 g)	110	6	49	1	8	30
Tuna, Chunk Light (in water), Bumble Bee, 2 oz. (56 g)	60	<1	8	0	0	30
Whiting, Fillets, Schooner, 3 oz. (85 g)	160	5	28	1	6	25

Frozen Appetizers & Entrées

FOOD/PORTION SIZE	CAL.	FAT Total (g)	FAT As % of Cal.	SAT. FAT Total (g)	SAT. FAT As % of Cal.	CHOL. (mg)
APPETIZERS						
Chicken Broccoli & Cheddar Pocket Sandwich, Weight Watchers, 1 sandwich (140 g)	250	6	22	<3	9	25
MEAT ENTRÉES						
Lasagne with Meat & Sauce, Stouffer's, 1 cup (215 g)	260	10	35	4	14	35
Pizza, Cheese Party, Totino's, ½ pizza (139 g)	320	14	39	5	14	20
Pizza, Cheese, Sausage and Mushroom, Tombstone Original, (12 inch) ⅕ pizza (129 g)	320	16	45	7	20	30

FOOD/PORTION SIZE	CAL.	FAT		SAT. FAT		CHOL. (mg)
		Total (g)	As % of Cal.	Total (g)	As % of Cal.	
Pizza, Deluxe French Bread, Lean Cuisine, 6.2 oz.	350	11	28	4	8	30
Pizza, Sausage, Pepperoni, & Mushroom, Stouffer's French Bread Deluxe, 1 pizza (175 g)	440	22	45	7	14	35
Pizza, Vegetable, Tombstone Light, ⅕ pizza (131 g)	240	7	26	<3	9	10
Pot Pie, Beef, Swanson, 1 pkg. (198 g)	380	19	45	8	19	30
Ravioli, Baked Cheese, Lean Cuisine, (240 g)	250	8	29	3	11	55
Salisbury Steak Dinner, Traditional, Healthy Choice, 1 meal	320	6	17	3	8	45
Salisbury Steak, Hungry Man, Swanson, 1 pkg. (461 g)	610	34	50	17	25	80
Salisbury Steak, Lean Cuisine, 1 pkg. (269 g)	240	7	26	2	8	45
Spaghetti, with meat sauce, Lean Cuisine, 1 pkg. (326 g)	290	6	19	<2	5	20
Szechwan Beef with Noodles, Lean Cuisine, 8⅝ oz.	259	9	31	3	10	83
MISCELLANEOUS						
Angel Hair Pasta, Weight Watcher Smart Ones, 1 entrée (242 g)	150	1	6	0	0	0
Cheddar Bake with Pasta & Vegetables, Lean Cuisine, 1 pkg. (255 g)	220	6	25	2	8	20
Cheese Ravioli, Lean Cuisine, 1 entrée (240 g)	250	8	29	3	11	55
Chicken Noodle Dinner, On-Cor, 1 cup (151 g)	140	5	32	2	13	15

FROZEN APPETIZERS & ENTRÉES

FOOD/PORTION SIZE	CAL.	FAT Total (g)	FAT As % of Cal.	SAT. FAT Total (g)	SAT. FAT As % of Cal.	CHOL. (mg)
Fettucini Primavera, Lean Cuisine, 1 entrée (283 g)	260	8	28	<3	9	35
Lasagne, Classic Cheese, Lean Cuisine, 1 container (326 g)	290	6	19	3	9	30
Macaroni & Cheese, Lean Cuisine, 1 cup (225 g)	330	17	46	6	16	30
Pasta Classic, Healthy Choice, 12½ oz.	310	3	9	tr	na	35
Rice & Chicken Stirfry, Lean Cuisine, 1 entrée (255 g)	280	9	29	1	3	15
Vegetable Pasta Italiano, Healthy Choice, 1 entrée (283 g)	220	1	4	0	0	0

POULTRY ENTRÉES

FOOD/PORTION SIZE	CAL.	FAT Total (g)	FAT As % of Cal.	SAT. FAT Total (g)	SAT. FAT As % of Cal.	CHOL. (mg)
Bow Tie Pasta & Chicken, Lean Cuisine (269 g)	270	6	20	<2	5	60
Chicken, Grilled Suiza with Rice, Weight Watchers (243 g)	240	6	23	2	8	35
Chicken Mirabella, Weight Watchers, Smart Ones (260 g)	160	1	6	<1	<5	10
Chicken Dijon Dinner, Healthy Choice, 1 meal	280	4	13	<2	5	30
Chicken Fettucini, Weight Watchers, 1 meal (233 g)	280	9	29	3	10	40
Chicken, French Recipe, Budget Gourmet Light and Healthy, 10 oz.	200	8	36	3	14	30
Chicken Parmigiana Dinner, Healthy Choice, 1 meal	300	<2	5	<1	2	35
Chicken, Sweet & Sour, Lean Cuisine (294 g)	260	<3	9	1	3	45

FOOD/PORTION SIZE	CAL.	FAT Total (g)	As % of Cal.	SAT. FAT Total (g)	As % of Cal.	CHOL. (mg)
Mesquite Chicken Dinner, Healthy Choice, 1 meal	320	2	6	<1	1	35
Pot Pie, Chicken, Swanson, 1 pkg. (198 g)	390	22	51	9	21	30
SEAFOOD ENTRÉES						
Filet of Fish Divan, Lean Cuisine, 1 pkg. (294 g)	210	6	26	1	4	65
Fish Fillets, Breaded, Hot & Spicy Gorton's, 2 fillets (104 g)	270	17	57	5	17	30
Fish Fillet Florentine, Booth, 9½ oz.	260	8	28	na	na	82
Pasta & Tuna Casserole, Lean, Cuisine, 1 entrée (272 g)	280	6	19	2	6	20
Shrimp & Vegetables Maria, Healthy Choice, 1 entrée (354 g)	260	2	7	<1	2	35
Shrimp Marinara, Weight Watchers, Smart Ones, 1 entrée (255 g)	190	2	9	<1	2	40
Shrimp Mariner, Budget Gourmet Light and Healthy, 11 oz.	260	6	21	2	7	60

Frozen Desserts

FOOD/PORTION SIZE	CAL.	FAT Total (g)	As % of Cal.	SAT. FAT Total (g)	As % of Cal.	CHOL. (mg)
DAIRY						
Ice Cream, Butter Pecan, Breyers, ½ cup (70 g)	180	12	60	6	30	35
Ice Cream, Cherry Garcia, Ben & Jerry, ½ cup	250	16	58	10	36	75

FROZEN DESSERTS

FOOD/PORTION SIZE	CAL.	FAT Total (g)	FAT As % of Cal.	SAT. FAT Total (g)	SAT. FAT As % of Cal.	CHOL. (mg)
Ice Cream, Chocolate, Breyers, ½ cup (70 g)	160	8	45	6	34	30
Ice Cream, Chocolate Fudge, Nonfat, Edy's Grand, ½ cup	100	0	0	0	0	0
Ice Cream, Strawberry, Natural, Breyers, ½ cup (70 g)	130	6	42	4	28	25
Ice Cream, Vanilla, Häagen-Dazs, ½ cup	270	18	60	11	37	120
Ice Cream, Vanilla, Natural, Breyers, ½ cup (70 g)	150	8	48	6	36	35
Ice Cream, Vanilla, Sealtest, ½ cup	140	7	45	5	32	na
Ice Cream, Vanilla/ Chocolate/Strawberry, Sealtest, ½ cup	140	6	39	na	na	na
Ice milk, vanilla, hardened, 1 cup	185	6	29	4	19	18
Ice milk, vanilla, soft serve, 1 cup	225	5	20	3	12	13
Sherbet, 1 cup	270	4	13	2	7	14
Sherbet, Raspberry Real Fruit, Dean Foods, ½ cup	110	1	7	na	na	na
Sorbet, Chunky, Real Fruit, Georgia Peach, ½ cup	100	0	0	0	0	0
Sorbet, Mango Fruit, Häagen-Dazs, ½ cup	120	0	0	0	0	0
SPECIALTY BARS						
Cappuccino, Iced, Häagen-Dazs Exträas, 1 bar	330	22	60	13	35	60
Chocolate with Dark Chocolate, Dove, 1 bar	270	17	57	11	37	30
Cone, Vanilla Fudge Sundae, Edy's Grand, 1 bar	340	19	50	11	29	30

FOOD/PORTION SIZE	CAL.	FAT Total (g)	FAT As % of Cal.	SAT. FAT Total (g)	SAT. FAT As % of Cal.	CHOL. (mg)
Cookies & Cream, Edy's Grand, 1 bar	260	17	59	9	31	25
Fruit Bars, all flavors, Edy's, 1 bar	90	0	0	0	0	0
Fruit Juice Bars, Light, all flavors, Welch's, 1 bar	25	0	0	0	0	0
Pudding Snacks, Chocolate, Jell-O, 1 snack (113 g)	160	5	28	2	11	0
Pudding Snacks, Chocolate, Jell-O Free, 1 snack (113 g)	100	0	0	0	0	0
Sandwich Bar, Vanilla, Lowfat, Weight Watchers, 1 sandwich	160	<4	23	2	11	5
Vanilla & Almond, Good Humor, Classics, 1 bar	190	9	43	4	19	10
Vanilla with Dark Chocolate, Dove, 1 bar	260	17	59	11	38	30
Vanilla with Dark Chocolate Coating, Eskimo Pie, 1 bar (3 fl. oz.)	180	12	60	na	na	na
Vanilla & Milk Chocolate, Good Humor, Classics, 1 bar	190	10	47	8	38	15

Fruit

FOOD/PORTION SIZE	CAL.	FAT Total (g)	FAT As % of Cal.	SAT. FAT Total (g)	SAT. FAT As % of Cal.	CHOL. (mg)
Apples, dried, sulfured, 10 rings	155	tr	na	tr	na	0
Apples, raw, unpeeled, 3¼-in. diameter, 1 apple	125	1	7	<1	tr	0
Apple Sauce, Canned, Original or *Chunky, Mott's*, 1 cup	90	0	0	0	0	0

FRUIT

FOOD/PORTION SIZE	CAL.	FAT Total (g)	FAT As % of Cal.	SAT. FAT Total (g)	SAT. FAT As % of Cal.	CHOL. (mg)
Applesauce, canned, sweetened, 1 cup	195	tr	na	<1	tr	0
Applesauce, canned, unsweetened, 1 cup	105	tr	na	tr	na	0
Apricot nectar, canned, 1 cup	140	tr	na	tr	na	0
Apricots, canned, heavy syrup pack, 3 halves	70	tr	na	tr	na	0
Apricots, canned, juice pack, 3 halves	40	tr	na	tr	na	0
Apricots, dried, cooked, unsweetened, 1 cup	210	tr	na	tr	na	0
Apricots, dried, uncooked, 1 cup	310	1	3	tr	na	0
Apricots, raw, 3 apricots	50	tr	na	tr	na	0
Avocados, raw, whole, California, 1 avocado	305	28	83	5	15	0
Avocados, raw, whole, Florida, 1 avocado	340	23	61	5	13	0
Bananas, raw, 1 banana	105	1	9	<1	2	0
Blackberries, raw, 1 cup	75	1	12	<1	2	0
Blueberries, frozen, sweetened, 10 oz.	230	tr	na	tr	na	0
Blueberries, raw, 1 cup	80	1	11	tr	na	0
Cantaloupe, raw, ½ melon	95	1	9	<1	<1	0
Cherries, sour, red, pitted, canned waterpack, 1 cup	90	tr	na	<1	1	0
Cherries, sweet, raw, 10 cherries	50	1	18	<1	2	0
Cranberry sauce, sweetened, canned, strained, 1 cup	420	tr	na	tr	na	0
Dates, chopped, ½ cup	245	<1	2	<1	<1	0
Dates, whole, w/o pits, 10 dates	230	tr	na	<1	<1	0
Figs, dried, 10 figs	475	2	4	<1	<1	0

FOOD/PORTION SIZE	CAL.	FAT Total (g)	FAT As % of Cal.	SAT. FAT Total (g)	SAT. FAT As % of Cal.	CHOL. (mg)
Fruit, Mixed, Libby's Chunky, Lite, ½ cup (123 g)	60	0	0	0	0	0
Fruit Cocktail, Del Monte, ½ cup (127 g)	100	0	0	0	0	0
Fruit Cocktail, Del Monte Lite, ½ cup (124 g)	60	0	0	0	0	0
Fruit Cocktail, Libby's Lite, ½ cup (123 g)	60	0	0	0	0	0
Grapefruit, canned, with syrup, 1 cup	150	tr	na	tr	na	0
Grapefruit, raw, ½ grapefruit	40	tr	na	tr	na	0
Grapes, Thompson seedless, 10 grapes	35	tr	na	<1	3	0
Grapes, Tokay/Emperor, seeded, 10 grapes	40	tr	na	<1	2	0
Honeydew melon, raw, ¹⁄₁₀ melon	45	tr	na	tr	na	0
Kiwifruit, raw, w/o skin, 1 kiwifruit	45	tr	na	tr	na	0
Lemons, raw, 1 lemon	15	tr	na	tr	na	0
Mangos, raw, 1 mango	135	1	7	<1	<1	0
Nectarines, raw, 1 nectarine	65	1	14	<1	1	0
Olives, canned, green, 4 medium or 3 extra large	15	2	100	<1	12	0
Olives, ripe, mission, pitted, 3 small or 2 large	15	2	100	<1	18	0
Oranges, raw, whole, w/o peel and seeds, 1 orange	60	tr	na	tr	na	0
Papayas, raw, ½-in. cubes, 1 cup	65	tr	na	<1	1	0
Peaches, canned, heavy syrup, 1 cup	190	tr	na	tr	na	0
Peaches, canned, juice pack, 1 cup	110	tr	na	tr	na	0

FRUIT

FOOD/PORTION SIZE	CAL.	FAT Total (g)	FAT As % of Cal.	SAT. FAT Total (g)	SAT. FAT As % of Cal.	CHOL. (mg)
Peaches, dried, uncooked, 1 cup	380	1	2	<1	<1	0
Peaches, frozen, sliced, sweetened, 1 cup	235	tr	na	tr	na	0
Peaches, raw, whole, 2½-in. diameter, 1 peach	35	tr	na	tr	na	0
Peaches, Sliced, Natural Lite, Libby's, ½ cup (124 g)	60	0	0	0	0	0
Pears, Bartlett raw, with skin, 1 pear	100	1	9	tr	na	0
Pears, Bosc raw, with skin, 1 pear	85	1	11	tr	na	0
Pears, canned, heavy syrup, 1 cup	190	tr	na	tr	na	0
Pears, canned, juice pack, 1 cup	125	tr	na	tr	na	0
Pears, D'Anjou raw, with skin, 1 pear	120	1	8	tr	na	0
Pears, Halves, Natural Lite, Libby's, ½ cup (124 g)	60	0	0	0	0	0
Pineapple, canned, heavy syrup, sliced, 1 slice	45	tr	na	tr	na	0
Pineapple, Canned, Heavy Syrup (all cuts), Dole, ½ cup	91	0	0	0	0	0
Pineapple, Canned, Juice Pack (all cuts), Dole, ½ cup	70	0	0	0	0	0
Pineapple, canned, juice pack slices, 1 slice	35	tr	na	tr	na	0
Pineapple, raw, diced, 1 cup	75	1	12	tr	na	0
Plums, canned, purple, juice pack, 3 plums	55	tr	na	tr	na	0
Plums, raw, 1½-in. diameter, 1 plum	15	tr	na	tr	na	0

FOOD/PORTION SIZE	CAL.	FAT Total (g)	FAT As % of Cal.	SAT. FAT Total (g)	SAT. FAT As % of Cal.	CHOL. (mg)
Plums, raw, 2⅛-in. diameter, 1 plum	35	tr	na	tr	na	0
Prunes, dried, cooked, unsweetened, 1 cup	225	tr	na	tr	na	0
Prunes, dried, uncooked, 4 extra large or 5 large	115	tr	na	tr	na	0
Raisins, seedless, 1 cup	435	1	12	<1	<1	0
Raisins, seedless, Dole, ½ cup (85 g)	250	0	0	0	0	0
Raspberries, frozen, sweetened, 1 cup	255	tr	na	tr	na	0
Raspberries, in Lite Syrup, Birds Eye Quick Thaw Pouch, 5 oz.	100	1	9	na	na	0
Raspberries, raw, 1 cup	60	1	15	tr	na	0
Rhubarb, cooked, added sugar, 1 cup	280	tr	na	tr	na	0
Strawberries, frozen, sweetened, sliced, 1 cup	245	tr	na	tr	na	0
Strawberries, Halved, in Lite Syrup, Birds Eye Quick Thaw Pouch, 5 oz.	90	0	0	0	0	0
Strawberries, Halved, in Syrup, Birds Eye Quick Thaw Pouch, 5 oz.	120	tr	na	tr	na	0
Strawberries, raw, whole, 1 cup	45	1	20	tr	na	0
Tangerine, canned, light syrup, 1 cup	155	tr	na	tr	na	0
Tangerine, raw, 2⅜-in. diameter, 1 tangerine	35	tr	na	tr	na	0
Watermelon, raw, 4 x 8-in. wedge, 1 piece	155	2	12	<1	2	0
Watermelon, raw, diced, 1 cup	50	1	18	<1	2	0

Gelatin, Pudding & Pie Filling

FOOD/PORTION SIZE	CAL.	FAT Total (g)	FAT As % of Cal.	SAT. FAT Total (g)	SAT. FAT As % of Cal.	CHOL (mg)
All flavors, Gelatin, Jell-O, ¼ pkg. (22 g)	80	0	0	0	0	0
All flavors, Gelatin, Sugar Free, Jell-O, ½ cup (average) ¼ pkg. (25 g)	10	0	0	0	0	0
Banana, Pudding & Pie Filling, Instant, Sugar Free Jell-O, with 2% milk, ½ cup	80	2	23	1	11	10
Banana Cream, Pudding & Pie Filling, Instant, Jell-O, with whole milk, ½ cup	160	4	23	3	17	15
Banana Cream, Pudding & Pie Filling, Jell-O, with whole milk, ⅙ pie (excluding crust)	100	3	27	2	18	10
Butterscotch, Pudding & Pie Filling, Instant, Jell-O, with whole milk, ½ cup	160	4	23	3	17	15
Butterscotch, Pudding & Pie Filling, Instant, Sugar Free, Jell-O, with 2% milk, ½ cup	90	2	20	1	10	10
Butterscotch, Pudding & Pie Filling, Jell-O, with whole milk, ½ cup	170	4	21	3	16	15
Chocolate, pudding, canned, 5-oz. can	205	11	48	9	40	1
Chocolate, Pudding & Pie Filling, Instant, Jell-O, with whole milk, ½ cup	180	4	20	3	15	15
Chocolate, Pudding & Pie Filling, Instant, Sugar Free, Jell-O, with 2% milk, ½ cup	90	3	30	2	20	10

GELATIN, PUDDING & PIE FILLING

FOOD/PORTION SIZE	CAL.	FAT Total (g)	FAT As % of Cal.	SAT. FAT Total (g)	SAT. FAT As % of Cal.	CHOL. (mg)
Chocolate, Pudding & Pie Filling, Jell-O, with whole milk, ½ cup	160	4	23	2	11	15
Chocolate, Pudding & Pie Filling, Sugar Free, Jell-O, with 2% milk, ½ cup	90	3	30	2	20	10
Chocolate Fudge, Pudding & Pie Filling, Jell-O, dry mix, ¼ pkg. (25 g)	90	0	0	0	0	10
Coconut Cream, Instant Pudding & Pie Filling, Jell-O, with whole milk, ½ cup	180	6	30	4	20	15
Coconut Cream, Pudding & Pie Filling, Jell-O, with whole milk, ⅙ pie (excluding crust)	110	4	33	2	16	10
Custard, Golden Egg, Mix, Jell-O Americana, with whole milk, ½ cup	160	5	28	3	17	80
Lemon, Pudding & Pie Filling, Instant, Jell-O, with whole milk, ½ cup	170	4	21	3	16	15
Lemon, Pudding & Pie Filling, Jell-O, with whole milk, ⅙ pie (excluding crust)	170	2	11	na	na	90
Milk Chocolate, Pudding & Pie Filling, Instant, Jell-O, with whole milk, ½ cup	180	5	25	3	15	17
Milk Chocolate, Pudding & Pie Filling, Jell-O, with whole milk, ½ cup	160	4	23	2	11	17
Pistachio, Pudding & Pie Filling, Instant, Jell-O, with whole milk, ½ cup	170	5	26	3	16	17
Pistachio, Pudding & Pie Filling, Instant, Sugar Free, Jell-O, with 2% milk, ½ cup	100	3	27	2	3	10

GELATIN, PUDDING & PIE FILLING

FOOD/PORTION SIZE	CAL.	FAT Total (g)	FAT As % of Cal.	SAT. FAT Total (g)	SAT. FAT As % of Cal.	CHOL. (mg)
Rice Pudding, Jell-O Americana, with whole milk, ½ cup	170	4	21	2	11	17
Vanilla, French, Pudding & Pie Filling, Instant, Jell-O, with whole milk, ½ cup	160	4	23	2	11	17
Vanilla, French, Pudding & Pie Filling, Jell-O, with whole milk, ½ cup	170	4	21	3	16	17
Vanilla, pudding, canned, 5-oz. can	220	10	41	10	41	1
Vanilla, pudding, regular (cooked) dry mix, made with whole milk, ½ cup	145	4	25	2	12	15
Vanilla, Pudding & Pie Filling, Instant, Jell-O, with whole milk, ½ cup	170	4	21	3	16	17
Vanilla, Pudding & Pie Filling, Instant, Sugar Free, Jell-O, with 2% milk, ½ cup	90	2	20	1	10	9
Vanilla, Pudding & Pie Filling, Sugar Free, Jell-O, with 2% milk, ½ cup	80	2	23	0	0	10
Vanilla, Tapioca, Pudding, Jell-O Americana, with whole milk, ½ cup	160	4	23	3	17	17

Gravies & Sauces

FOOD/PORTION SIZE	CAL.	FAT Total (g)	FAT As % of Cal.	SAT. FAT Total (g)	SAT. FAT As % of Cal.	CHOL. (mg)
GRAVIES						
Beef, canned, 1 cup	125	5	36	3	22	7
Beef, Franco-American, ¼ cup (60 mL)	30	2	60	1	30	5

FOOD/PORTION SIZE	CAL.	FAT Total (g)	FAT As % of Cal.	SAT. FAT Total (g)	SAT. FAT As % of Cal.	CHOL. (mg)
Brown, from dry mix, 1 cup	80	2	23	1	11	2
Brown, with onions, Zesty, Homestyle, Heinz, ¼ cup (60 g)	20	<1	22	0	0	0
Chicken, canned, 1 cup	190	14	66	4	19	5
Chicken, Franco-American, ¼ cup (60 mL)	45	4	80	1	20	5
Chicken, from dry mix, 1 cup	85	2	21	<1	5	tr
Roasted Turkey, Heinz HomeStyle, ¼ cup (60 g)	25	1	36	0	0	0
SAUCES						
Barbecue sauce, see BAKING PRODUCTS & CONDIMENTS						
Cheese, from dry mix, prepared with milk, 1 cup	305	17	50	9	27	53
Hollandaise, prepared with water, 2 tbsp.	30	3	90	2	60	7
Picante Sauce, Old El Paso, 2 tbsp. (30 g)	10	0	0	0	0	0
Picante Sauce, Pace, 2 tbsp. (31.5 g)	10	0	0	0	0	0
Soy sauce, see BAKING PRODUCTS & CONDIMENTS						
Spaghetti, Chunky Garden Style, with Mushrooms and Green Peppers, Ragu, ½ cup (128 g)	120	4	30	<1	4	0
Spaghetti, Extra Chunky, Mushrooms & Diced Tomatoes, Prego, ½ cup (120 mL)	110	4	33	1	8	0
Spaghetti, Extra Chunky, Tomato, Onion & Garlic, Prego, ½ cup (120 mL)	120	6	45	<2	11	0

GRAVIES & SAUCES

FOOD/PORTION SIZE	CAL.	FAT Total (g)	FAT As % of Cal.	SAT. FAT Total (g)	SAT. FAT As % of Cal.	CHOL. (mg)
Spaghetti, Plain, Prego, ½ cup (120 mL)	150	6	36	2	12	0
Spaghetti, Ragu, ½ cup (125 mL)	80	<4	39	<1	6	0
Spaghetti, Traditional, Old World Style, Ragu, ½ cup (125 g)	80	<4	39	<1	6	0
Spaghetti, with Meat, Prego, ½ cup (120 mL)	160	6	34	<2	8	5
Spaghetti, with Meat, Ragu, 4 oz.	80	3	34	tr	na	2
Spaghetti, with Fresh Mushrooms, Prego, ½ cup (120 mL)	150	5	30	<2	9	0
Spaghetti, with Mushrooms, Old World Style, Ragu, ½ cup (125 g)	80	<4	39	<1	6	0
Spaghetti, with Mushrooms, Thick & Hearty, Ragu, 4 oz.	140	5	32	tr	na	0
White, prepared with milk, 1 cup	240	13	49	6	23	36

Legumes & Nuts

FOOD/PORTION SIZE	CAL.	FAT Total (g)	FAT As % of Cal.	SAT. FAT Total (g)	SAT. FAT As % of Cal.	CHOL. (mg)
BEANS						
Black, dry, cooked, drained, 1 cup	225	1	4	<1	<1	0
Chickpeas, dry, cooked, drained, 1 cup	270	4	13	<1	1	0
Lentils, dry, cooked, 1 cup	215	1	4	<1	<1	0
Lima, dry, cooked, drained, 1 cup	216	1	4	<1	<1	0

FOOD/PORTION SIZE	CAL.	FAT Total (g)	FAT As % of Cal.	SAT. FAT Total (g)	SAT. FAT As % of Cal.	CHOL. (mg)
Lima, immature seeds, frozen, cooked, drained: thick-seeded types (Ford-hooks), 1 cup	170	1	5	<1	<1	0
Lima, immature seeds, frozen, cooked, drained: thin-seeded types (baby limas), 1 cup	188	1	5	<1	<1	0
Peas (navy), dry, cooked, drained, 1 cup	225	1	4	<1	<1	0
Pinto, dry, cooked, drained, 1 cup	265	1	3	<1	<1	0
Pork and Beans, Van Camp's, ½ cup (130 g)	110	<2	12	<1	4	0
Red kidney, canned, 1 cup	230	1	4	<1	<1	0
Refried, canned, 1 cup	268	3	10	1	3	15
Refried, Fat Free, Old El Paso, ½ cup (124 g)	110	0	0	0	0	0
Refried, Vegetarian, Old El Paso, 1 cup	140	2	13	na	na	0
Snap, canned, drained, solids (cut), 1 cup	25	tr	na	tr	na	0
Snap, cooked, drained, from frozen (cut), 1 cup	35	tr	na	tr	na	0
Snap, cooked, drained, from raw (cut and French style), 1 cup	45	tr	na	<1	2	0
Sprouts (mung), raw, 1 cup	30	tr	na	tr	na	0
Tahini, 1 tbsp.	95	7	66	1	9	0
White, with sliced frankfurters, canned, 1 cup	365	18	44	7	17	30

LEGUMES & NUTS

FOOD/PORTION SIZE	CAL.	FAT Total (g)	FAT As % of Cal.	SAT. FAT Total (g)	SAT. FAT As % of Cal.	CHOL. (mg)
NUTS						
Almonds, shelled, whole, 1 oz.	165	15	82	1	5	0
Almonds, sliced, 1 oz.	170	13	69	1	5	0
Brazil, shelled, 1 oz.	185	19	92	4	19	0
Cashew, salted, dry roasted, 1 cup	869	65	67	14	14	0
Cashew, salted, roasted in oil, 1 cup	869	67	69	14	14	0
Chestnuts, European, roasted, shelled, 1 cup	350	3	8	tr	na	0
Coconut, raw, piece, 1.6 oz. (45 g)	160	15	84	13	73	0
Filberts (hazelnuts), chopped, 1 cup	955	84	79	7	7	0
Macadamia, salted, roasted in oil, 1 cup	1088	103	85	16	13	0
Mixed, with peanuts, salted, dry roasted, 1 oz.	170	13	69	2	11	0
Mixed, with peanuts, salted, roasted in oil, 1 oz.	175	14	72	2	10	0
Peanut Butter, Creamy, Skippy, 2 tbsp. (32 g)	190	17	81	3	14	0
Peanut Butter, Extra Crunchy, Jif, 2 tbsp. (32 g)	190	16	76	3	14	0
Peanuts, Dry Roasted, Planter's, about 39 peanuts, 1 oz. (28 g)	160	13	73	2	11	0
Peanuts, salted, roasted in oil, 1 cup	869	64	66	9	9	0
Pecans, halves, 1 cup	760	68	81	6	7	0
Pistachio, dried, shelled, 1 oz.	165	13	71	2	11	0
Walnuts, black, chopped, 1 cup	760	62	73	4	5	0
Walnuts, English or Persian, pieces/chips, 1 cup	770	66	77	6	7	0

FOOD/PORTION SIZE	CAL.	FAT Total (g)	FAT As % of Cal.	SAT. FAT Total (g)	SAT. FAT As % of Cal.	CHOL. (mg)
PEAS						
Black-eyed, dry, cooked, 1 cup	190	1	5	<1	1	0
Split, dry, cooked, 1 cup	230	1	4	<1	<1	0
SEEDS						
Pumpkin/squash kernels, dry, hulled, 1 oz.	155	13	75	2	12	0
Sesame, dry, hulled, 1 tbsp.	45	4	80	<1	12	0
Sunflower, dry, hulled, 1 oz.	160	14	79	<2	8	0
SOY PRODUCTS						
Miso, 1 cup	568	14	22	2	3	0
Soybeans, dry, cooked, drained, 1 cup	298	13	39	2	6	0
Tofu, firm, 2 oz.	82	5	55	tr	na	0

Meats

FOOD/PORTION SIZE	CAL.	FAT Total (g)	FAT As % of Cal.	SAT. FAT Total (g)	SAT. FAT As % of Cal.	CHOL. (mg)
BEEF						
Chipped, dried, 2½ oz.	118	3	23	1	8	50
Chuck blade, lean only, braised/simmered/pot roasted, approx. 2¼ oz.	168	9	48	4	21	66
Corned, canned, 3 oz.	213	16	68	5	21	83
Corned, Lean, Carl Buddig, 10 slices (55 g)	75	4	48	<2	18	40
Ground, patty, broiled, regular, 3 oz.	245	18	66	7	26	76
Ground, patty, lean, broiled, 3 oz.	230	16	63	6	27	74
Heart, lean, braised, 3 oz.	150	5	30	2	12	164

MEATS

FOOD/PORTION SIZE	CAL.	FAT Total (g)	FAT As % of Cal.	SAT. FAT Total (g)	SAT. FAT As % of Cal.	CHOL. (mg)
Liver, fried, 3 oz.	185	7	34	3	15	410
Roast, eye of round, lean only, oven cooked, approx. 2½ oz.	135	5	33	2	13	52
Roast, rib, lean only, oven cooked, approx. 2¼ oz.	150	9	54	4	24	49
Round, bottom, lean only, braised/simmered/pot roasted, 24.5 oz.	175	8	41	3	15	75
Steak, sirloin, lean only, broiled, 2½ oz.	150	6	36	3	18	64
FRANKS & SAUSAGES						
Franks, Healthy Choice, 1 frank (57 g)	70	<2	19	<1	6	20
Franks, Beef, Healthy Choice, 1 frank (50 g)	60	<2	23	<1	8	30
Franks, Beef, Oscar Mayer, 1 link (45 g)	150	13	78	6	36	25
Franks, Jumbo, Eckrich, 1 frank (57 g)	180	17	85	6	30	35
Franks, Jumbo Beef, Eckrich, 1 frank (57 g)	190	17	81	7	33	35
Franks, Turkey, Butterball, 1 frank (45 g)	100	8	72	<4	32	35
Sausage, beef and pork, frankfurters, cooked, 1 frank	183	16	79	6	30	29
Sausage, pork, brown/serve, browned, 1 link	50	5	90	2	36	9
Sausage, pork, links, 1 link (1 oz.)	50	4	72	2	36	11
Sausage, Pork, Regular, Jimmy Dean, 2 oz. cooked (56 g)	250	24	86	8	30	50
Weiners, Oscar Mayer, 1 link (45 g)	150	13	78	5	30	30

FOOD/PORTION SIZE	CAL.	FAT Total (g)	FAT As % of Cal.	SAT. FAT Total (g)	SAT. FAT As % of Cal.	CHOL. (mg)
GAME						
Buffalo, roasted, 3 oz.	111	2	16	<1	na	52
Venison, roasted, 3 oz.	134	3	20	1	7	95
LAMB						
Chops, shoulder, lean only, braised, approx. 1¾ oz.	135	7	47	3	20	44
Leg, lean only, roasted, approx. 2⅔ oz.	140	6	39	3	19	65
Loin, chop, lean only, broiled, approx. 2⅓ oz.	182	10	49	4	20	60
Rib, lean only, roasted, 2 oz.	130	7	48	4	28	50
LUNCHEON MEATS						
Bologna, Beef, Oscar Mayer, 1 slice (28 g)	90	8	80	4	40	15
Bologna, Lite, Oscar Mayer, 1 slice (28 g)	50	4	72	<2	27	15
Bologna, Oscar Mayer, 1 slice (28 g)	90	8	80	3	30	20
Braunschweiger sausage, 2 oz.	205	18	79	7	31	88
Chicken, roll, light, 2 oz.	90	4	40	1	10	28
Ham, chopped, 8-slice pack, 2 slices (1½ oz.)	98	7	64	3	28	23
Ham, extra lean, cooked, 2 slices (2 oz.)	75	3	36	1	12	27
Ham, regular, cooked, 2 slices (2 oz.)	105	6	51	2	17	32
Pork, canned lunch meat, spiced/unspiced, 2 slices, 1½ oz. (42 g)	140	13	84	5	32	26
Salami sausage, cooked, 2 oz.	141	11	70	5	32	37

MEATS

FOOD/PORTION SIZE	CAL.	FAT Total (g)	FAT As % of Cal.	SAT. FAT Total (g)	SAT. FAT As % of Cal.	CHOL. (mg)
Salami sausage, dry, 12-slice pack, 2 slices (⅔ oz.)	84	6	64	2	21	16
Sandwich spread, pork/beef, 1 tbsp.	35	3	77	<1	23	6
Turkey Bologna, Louis Rich Turkey Cold Cuts, 1 slice (28 g)	50	4	72	1	18	20
Turkey Breast, Healthy Choice, 6 slices, (54 g)	60	<2	23	<1	8	25
Turkey, breast meat, loaf, 8-slice pack, 2 slices (1½ oz.)	45	1	20	<1	4	17
Turkey, Breast, Roasted, Oscar Mayer, 4 slices (52 g)	50	1	18	0	0	20
Turkey, thigh meat, ham cured, 2 oz.	75	3	36	1	12	32
Turkey Ham, Louis Rich Turkey Cold Cuts, 1 slice (28 g)	35	1	26	0	0	20
Turkey Salami, Louis Rich, 1 slice (28 g)	45	<3	50	1	20	20
Vienna sausage, 7 per 4-oz. can, 1 sausage, approx. ½ oz. (16 g)	45	4	80	2	40	8

PORK

FOOD/PORTION SIZE	CAL.	FAT Total (g)	FAT As % of Cal.	SAT. FAT Total (g)	SAT. FAT As % of Cal.	CHOL. (mg)
Bacon, Canadian, cured, cooked, 2 slices	86	4	42	1	10	27
Bacon, regular, cured, cooked, 3 medium slices	108	9	75	3	25	16
Chop, loin, fresh, lean only, broiled, 2½ oz.	163	7	39	3	17	69
Chop, loin, fresh, lean only, pan fried, approx. 2½ oz.	181	10	50	4	20	73
Ham, Boiled, Oscar Mayer, 3 slices (63 g)	70	2	26	<1	6	35

FOOD/PORTION SIZE	CAL.	FAT Total (g)	FAT As % of Cal.	SAT. FAT Total (g)	SAT. FAT As % of Cal.	CHOL. (mg)
Ham, canned, roasted, 3 oz.	140	7	45	2	13	35
Ham, leg, fresh, lean only, roasted, 2½ oz.	156	8	46	3	17	67
Ham, light cure, lean only, roasted, approx. 2½ oz.	107	4	34	1	8	38
Rib, fresh, lean only, roasted, 2½ oz.	173	8	42	3	16	56
Shoulder cut, fresh, lean only, braised, 2²/₅ oz.	169	8	43	3	16	78
Tenderloin, roasted, lean, 3 oz.	139	4	26	1	6	67
Turkey Bacon, Louis Rich, 1 slice (14 g)	30	<3	75	<1	15	10
VEAL						
Cubed, lean only, braised, 3½ oz.	188	4	19	1	5	145
Cutlet, leg, lean only, braised, 3½ oz.	203	6	27	2	9	135
Rib, lean only, roasted, 3½ oz.	177	7	36	2	10	115

Packaged Entrées

FOOD/PORTION SIZE	CAL.	FAT Total (g)	FAT As % of Cal.	SAT. FAT Total (g)	SAT. FAT As % of Cal.	CHOL. (mg)
Beef Noodle, Hamburger Helper, 1 cup, prepared (from 34 g mix)	120	<2	11	0	0	25
Beef Stew, Dinty Moore (284 g)	300	13	39	5	15	40
Cheeseburger Macaroni, Hamburger Helper, 1 cup, prepared (from 45 g mix)	170	5	26	2	11	5

PACKAGED ENTRÉES

FOOD/PORTION SIZE	CAL.	FAT Total (g)	FAT As % of Cal.	SAT. FAT Total (g)	SAT. FAT As % of Cal.	CHOL. (mg)
Chicken, Sweet & Sour, LaChoy, ¾ cup	230	2	8	tr	na	103
Chili con carne with beans, canned, 1 cup	286	13	41	6	19	43
Chow Mein, Beef, LaChoy, 1 cup (248 g)	80	1	11	0	0	10
Chow Mein, Chicken, LaChoy, 1 cup (245 g)	100	4	36	1	9	17
Egg Noodle and Cheese Dinner, Kraft, ¾ cup	340	17	45	4	11	50
Egg Noodle with Chicken Dinner, Kraft, ¾ cup	240	9	34	2	8	45
Lasagne, Hamburger Helper, prepared with meat, 1 cup (from 44 g mix)	310	11	32	4	12	55
Macaroni and Cheese Deluxe Dinner, Kraft, about 1 cup (98 g)	320	10	28	6	17	25
Macaroni and Cheese Dinner, Original, Kraft, about 1 cup (70 g)	260	3	9	1	3	10
Shells and Cheese Dinner, Velveeta, about 1 cup (126 g)	410	15	33	9	20	45
Spaghetti Dinner, Mild American Style, Kraft, prepared, about 1 cup (230 g)	270	<5	15	1	3	<5
Spaghetti Dinner, Tangy Italian Style, Kraft, about 1 cup (56 g)	270	3	10	<1	2	5
Spaghetti in tomato sauce with cheese, canned, 1 cup	190	2	9	<1	2	3

FOOD/PORTION SIZE	CAL.	FAT Total (g)	FAT As % of Cal.	SAT. FAT Total (g)	SAT. FAT As % of Cal.	CHOL. (mg)
Spaghetti with Meat Sauce, Top Shelf 2-Minute Entrée, Hormel, 10 oz.	260	6	21	na	na	20
Spaghetti with Meat Sauce Dinner, Kraft, prepared, about 1 cup (235 g)	330	11	30	4	11	15

Pasta

FOOD/PORTION SIZE	CAL.	FAT Total (g)	FAT As % of Cal.	SAT. FAT Total (g)	SAT. FAT As % of Cal.	CHOL. (mg)
Angel Hair, Di Giorno, 2 oz. (56 g)	160	1	6	0	0	0
Angel Hair Pasta w/Parmesan Cheese Sauce, Noodle Roni, prepared with margarine and 2% milk, 2 oz. (56 g) (¾-inch circle pasta and 1⅔ tbsp. sauce mix)	440	10	20	2	4	5
Dumpling Egg Noodles, Creamette, 1⅓ cups (56 g)	220	3	12	1	4	55
Egg Noodles Substitute, Cholesterol Free, No Yolks, 2 oz. dry (56 g)	210	<1	2	0	0	0
Fettucini, Noodle Roni, prepared with margarine and 2% milk, 2.5 oz. (70 g), (about 1 cup dry pasta & 3 tbsp. sauce mix)	550	12	20	3	5	5
Linguine, Di Giorno, 2.5 oz. (70 g)	190	<2	7	0	0	0
Macaroni, Elbows, Prince, ½ cup (56 g dry)	210	1	4	0	0	0

PASTA

FOOD/PORTION SIZE	CAL.	FAT Total (g)	FAT As % of Cal.	SAT. FAT Total (g)	SAT. FAT As % of Cal.	CHOL. (mg)
Macaroni, enriched, cooked, tender, cold, 1 cup	115	tr	na	<1	<1	0
Macaroni, enriched, cooked, tender, hot, 1 cup	155	1	6	<1	<1	0
Macaroni and cheese dishes, *see* PACKAGED ENTRÉES						
Noodles, chow mein, canned, 1 cup	220	11	45	2	8	5
Noodles, Chow Mein, China Boy, ½ cup (25 g)	125	5	36	1	7	0
Noodles, Creamette, all types except egg, ½ cup (56 g)	210	1	4	0	0	0
Noodles, egg, enriched, cooked, 1 cup	200	2	9	1	5	50
Ravioli with Italian Sausage, Di Giorno, ¾ cup (103 g)	340	12	32	5	13	50
Spaghetti, enriched, cooked, firm, hot, 1 cup	190	1	5	<1	<1	0
Spaghetti, Enriched No. 3, Prince, 2 oz. (56 g)	210	1	4	0	0	0
Spaghetti with sauce/meat, *see* PACKAGED ENTRÉES						
Tenderthin Pasta w/ Parmesan Sauce, Noodle Roni, prepared with margarine and 2% milk, 2.5 oz. (70 g) (about 1⅓ cups dry pasta and 2 tbsp. sauce mix)	400	17	39	<5	10	10
Vermicelli, Creamette, 2 oz. (dry)	210	1	4	0	0	0

Poultry

FOOD/PORTION SIZE	CAL.	FAT Total (g)	FAT As % of Cal.	SAT. FAT Total (g)	SAT. FAT As % of Cal.	CHOL. (mg)
Chicken, boneless, canned, 5 oz.	235	11	42	3	11	88
Chicken, breast, flesh only, roasted, 3 oz.	140	3	19	<1	6	73
Chicken, broiler-fryer, breast, w/o skin, roasted, 3½ oz.	165	4	22	1	5	85
Chicken, drumstick, roasted, approx. 1³/₅ oz.	75	2	24	<1	8	26
Chicken, light and dark meat, flesh only, stewed, 1 cup	332	17	46	1	3	117
Chicken, liver, cooked, 1 liver	30	1	30	<1	12	120
Chicken, white and dark meat, w/o skin, roasted, 3½ oz.	190	7	33	2	9	89
Cold cuts, chicken or turkey, *see* LUNCHEON MEATS in MEATS section						
Duck, flesh only, roast, ½ duck, approx. 7¾ oz.	445	24	49	11	22	197
Frankfurters, chicken, or turkey, *see* FRANKS & SAUSAGES in MEATS section						
Turkey, dark meat only, w/o skin, roast, 3½ oz.	187	7	34	2	10	85
Turkey, flesh only, 1 light and 2 dark slices (85 g, 3 oz.)	145	4	25	1	6	65
Turkey, flesh only, light and dark meat, chopped or diced, roasted, 1 cup (140 g, 5 oz.)	240	7	26	2	8	106
Turkey, flesh only, light meat, roasted, 2 pieces (85 g, 3 oz.)	135	3	20	1	7	59

POULTRY

FOOD/PORTION SIZE	CAL.	FAT Total (g)	FAT As % of Cal.	SAT. FAT Total (g)	SAT. FAT As % of Cal.	CHOL. (mg)
Turkey, frozen, boneless, light and dark meat, seasoned, chunked, roasted, 3 oz.	130	5	35	2	14	45
Turkey, patties, breaded, battered, fried, 1 patty	180	12	60	3	15	40
Turkey, white meat only, w/o skin, roasted, 3½ oz.	157	3	17	1	6	69
Turkey and gravy, frozen, 5 oz. pkg.	95	3	28	1	9	18

Rice

FOOD/PORTION SIZE	CAL.	FAT Total (g)	FAT As % of Cal.	SAT. FAT Total (g)	SAT. FAT As % of Cal.	CHOL. (mg)
Beef Flavor, Rice-A-Roni, prepared with margarine, 2.5 oz. (70 g)	320	<10	27	1	3	0
Brown, cooked, hot, 1 cup	230	1	4	<1	1	0
Brown & Wild, Mushroom Recipe, Uncle Ben's, ½ cup	130	1	7	na	na	0
Chicken Flavor, Rice-A-Roni, prepared with margarine, 2.5 oz. (70 g) (about ⅓ cup dry mix and 1 tbsp. seasoning mix)	400	8	18	1	2	0
Chicken, Rice-A-Roni, prepared with margarine, 2.5 oz. (70 g)	320	<10	27	1	3	0
Extra-Long-Grain, Riceland, ½ cup	100	0	0	0	0	0
Herb Rice Au Gratin, Country Inn Recipes, Uncle Ben's, prepared with margarine, ½ pkg., 2.5 oz. (70 g)	260	4	14	2	7	5

FOOD/PORTION SIZE	CAL.	FAT		SAT. FAT		CHOL. (mg)
		Total (g)	As % of Cal.	Total (g)	As % of Cal.	
Instant, ready-to-serve, hot, 1 cup	180	0	0	0	0	0
Long Grain & Wild, Original Recipe, Uncle Ben's, (about ½ cup cooked)	100	<1	<9	na	na	0
Long Grain & Wild, Rice-A-Roni, prepared with margarine, ½ cup	137	3	20	1	7	0
Long Grain, Natural, Converted, Uncle Ben's, ⅔ cup	120	0	0	0	0	0
Minute Rice, ½ cup (44 g)	170	0	0	0	0	0
Parboiled, cooked, hot, 1 cup	185	tr	na	tr	na	0
Parboiled, raw, 1 cup	685	1	1	<1	<1	0
Savory Broccoli Au Gratin, Rice-A-Roni, prepared with margarine, ½ cup	178	10	51	3	15	4
Savory Rice Pilaf, Rice-A-Roni, prepared with margarine, 2.5 oz. (70 g) (⅓ cup dry mix and 1 tbsp. seasoning mix)	380	8	19	1	2	0
White, enriched, cooked, hot, 1 cup	225	tr	na	<1	<1	0

Salad Dressings

FOOD/PORTION SIZE	CAL.	FAT		SAT. FAT		CHOL. (mg)
		Total (g)	As % of Cal.	Total (g)	As % of Cal.	
Bacon & Tomato, Kraft, 2 tbsp. (30 g)	140	14	90	<3	16	<5
Blue Cheese, Chunky, Seven Seas, 2 tbsp. (33 g)	90	7	70	4	40	10

SALAD DRESSINGS

FOOD/PORTION SIZE	CAL.	FAT Total (g)	FAT As % of Cal.	SAT. FAT Total (g)	SAT. FAT As % of Cal.	CHOL. (mg)
Blue Cheese Flavor, Fat Free, Kraft Free, 2 tbsp. (35 g)	50	0	0	0	0	0
Blue Cheese, Lite, Less Oil, Wish-Bone, 2 tbsp. (30 mL)	80	8	90	2	23	0
Buttermilk Ranch, Kraft, 2 tbsp. (29 g)	150	16	96	3	18	<5
Caesar, Weight Watchers, 2 tbsp. (30 g)	10	0	0	0	0	0
Caesar, Creamy Classic, Special Edition, Lawry's, 2 tbsp.	130	14	97	4	28	30
Caesar, Olive Oil, Wish-Bone Lite, 2 tbsp.	60	5	75	1	15	0
Catalina, Fat Free, Kraft, 2 tbsp. (35 g)	45	0	0	0	0	0
Catalina, French, Kraft, 2 tbsp. (34 g)	80	4	45	<1	6	0
Cheese Garlic, Good Seasons, with vinegar and oil, 1 tbsp.	7	8	100	na	na	0
Coleslaw, Kraft, 2 tbsp. (32 g)	150	12	72	2	12	25
Cucumber Ranch, Kraft, 2 tbsp. (30 g)	150	15	90	<3	15	0
Cucumber Ranch, Reduced Calorie, Kraft, 2 tbsp. (31 g)	60	5	75	1	15	0
Dijon, Honey, Wish-Bone, 2 tbsp.	130	10	69	<2	10	0
Dijon, Honey, Fat Free, Hidden Valley Ranch, 2 tbsp.	35	0	0	0	0	0
Dijon, Honey, Healthy Sensation, Wish-Bone, 2 tbsp.	45	0	0	0	0	0
French, Catalina Brand, Kraft, 2 tbsp. (32 g)	140	11	71	2	13	0

FOOD/PORTION SIZE	CAL.	FAT		SAT. FAT		CHOL. (mg)
		Total (g)	As % of Cal.	Total (g)	As % of Cal.	
French, Deluxe, Wish-Bone, 2 tbsp. (30 mL)	120	11	83	<2	11	0
French, Fat Free, Henri's, 2 tbsp.	45	0	0	0	0	0
French, Kraft, 2 tbsp. (31 g)	120	12	90	2	15	0
French, Light, Henri's, 2 tbsp.	70	2	26	0	0	0
French, No Oil, Pritikin, 2 tbsp. (32 g)	20	0	0	0	0	0
French, Reduced Calorie, Kraft Free, 2 tbsp. (35 g)	50	0	0	0	0	0
French, Sweet 'n Spicy Lite, Wish-Bone, 2 tbsp. (30 mL)	16	0	0	0	0	0
French, Weight Watchers, 2 tbsp. (30 g)	40	0	0	0	0	0
Garlic and Herbs, Good Seasons, with oil and vinegar, 1/8 envelope (2.5 g)	140	15	71	2	13	0
Garlic, Creamy, Kraft, 2 tbsp. (30 g)	110	11	90	2	16	0
Italian, Creamy, Reduced Calorie, Kraft, 2 tbsp. (31 g)	50	5	90	1	18	0
Italian Garlic, Creamy, Marie's, 2 tbsp.	180	19	95	3	15	10
Italian Herb, Creamy, Marie's Lowfat, 2 tbsp.	40	2	45	0	0	0
Italian, Good Seasons, with oil and vinegar, 1/8 envelope (2.5 g)	40	15	71	2	13	0
Italian, Fat Free, Good Seasons, prepared with vinegar and water, 2 tbsp.	20	0	0	0	0	0
Italian, Lite, Wish-Bone, 2 tbsp. (30 mL)	15	<1	30	0	0	0

SALAD DRESSINGS

FOOD/PORTION SIZE	CAL.	FAT Total (g)	FAT As % of Cal.	SAT. FAT Total (g)	SAT. FAT As % of Cal.	CHOL. (mg)
Italian, Mild, Good Seasons, with oil and vinegar, ⅛ envelope (3.5 g)	150	15	90	<3	15	0
Italian, Zesty, No Oil, Pritikin, 2 tbsp. (31 g)	20	0	0	0	0	0
Italian, Zesty, Good Seasons, with oil and vinegar, ⅛ envelope (2 g)	140	15	96	2	13	0
Italian, Zesty, Kraft, 2 tbsp. (30 g)	110	11	90	<2	12	0
Italian, Fat Free, Kraft, 2 tbsp. (31 g)	10	0	0	0	0	0
Lemon Pepper, Classic, Special Edition, Lawry's, 2 tbsp.	130	13	90	2	14	0
Miracle Whip, Free Nonfat, 1 tbsp. (16 g)	15	0	0	0	0	0
Miracle Whip Light, Light Dressing, 1 tbsp. (15 g)	40	3	68	0	0	0
Miracle Whip Salad Dressing, 1 tbsp. (14 g)	70	7	90	1	13	5
Ranch, Original, Hidden Valley Ranch, 2 tbsp. (30 g)	140	14	90	2	13	10
Ranch, Original, Low Fat, Hidden Valley Ranch, 1 tbsp.	40	2	45	0	0	0
Red Wine, Vinegar and Oil, Seven Seas, 2 tbsp.	110	11	90	2	16	0
Russian, Kraft, 2 tbsp. (33 g)	130	10	69	<2	10	0
Thousand Island, Kraft, 2 tbsp. (31 g)	110	10	82	<2	12	10
Thousand Island, Wish-Bone, 2 tbsp.	130	12	83	2	14	10
Thousand Island, Reduced Calorie, Fat Free, Kraft, 2 tbsp. (35 g)	45	0	0	0	0	0

FOOD/PORTION SIZE	CAL.	FAT Total (g)	FAT As % of Cal.	SAT. FAT Total (g)	SAT. FAT As % of Cal.	CHOL. (mg)
Vinaigrette, Blush, Classic, Special Edition, Lawry's, 2 tbsp.	170	13	69	2	11	na
Vinaigrette, Red Wine, Classic, Special Edition, Lawry's, 2 tbsp.	90	7	70	1	10	na

Snacks

FOOD/PORTION SIZE	CAL.	FAT Total (g)	FAT As % of Cal.	SAT. FAT Total (g)	SAT. FAT As % of Cal.	CHOL. (mg)
CORN CHIPS						
Bugles, 1½ cups (30 g)	160	9	51	8	45	0
Doritos, Cool Ranch, 1 oz., about 15 chips, (15 g)	140	7	45	1	6	0
Doritos, Nacho Cheese, 1 oz., about 15 chips, (15 g)	140	7	45	1	6	0
Fritos Corn Chips, 1 oz., about 32 chips (28 g)	160	10	56	<2	8	0
Tortilla Chips, No Oil, Guiltless Gourmet, about 22 chips (28 g)	110	<2	12	0	0	0
Tostitos, Traditional, 1 oz., about 24 chips (28 g)	140	8	51	1	6	0
DIPS						
Avocado (guacamole), Kraft, 2 tbsp.	50	4	72	2	36	0
Bacon & Horseradish, Kraft, 2 tbsp.	60	5	75	3	45	0
Blue Cheese, Kraft Premium, 2 tbsp.	50	4	72	2	36	10
Clam, Kraft, 2 tbsp.	60	4	60	1	15	10
Cucumber, Creamy, Kraft Premium, 2 tbsp.	50	4	72	3	54	10

SNACKS

FOOD/PORTION SIZE	CAL.	FAT Total (g)	FAT As % of Cal.	SAT. FAT Total (g)	SAT. FAT As % of Cal.	CHOL. (mg)
French Onion, Kraft, 2 tbsp.	60	4	60	2	30	0
Green Onion, Kraft, 2 tbsp.	60	4	60	2	30	0
Jalapeño Pepper, Kraft, 2 tbsp.	50	4	72	2	36	0
Nacho Cheese, Kraft Premium, 2 tbsp.	55	4	65	2	33	10
Onion, Creamy, Kraft Premium, 2 tbsp.	45	4	80	2	40	10
FRUIT SNACKS						
Apple Cinnamon, Pop-Tarts, Kellogg's, 1 pastry (52 g)	210	5	21	1	4	0
Blueberry, Frosted, Pop-Tarts, Kellogg's, 1 pastry (52 g)	200	5	23	1	5	0
Cherry, Frosted, Pop-Tarts, Kellogg's, 1 pastry (52 g)	200	5	23	1	5	0
Orange, Fruit Wrinkles, Betty Crocker, 1 pouch	100	2	18	tr	na	0
Strawberry, Fruit Wrinkles, Betty Crocker, 1 pouch	100	2	18	tr	na	0
Strawberry, Frosted, Pop-Tarts, Kellogg's, 1 pastry (52 g)	200	5	23	1	5	0
GRANOLA						
Caramel Apple, Chewy Granola Bar, Quaker Oats, 1 bar (28 g)	120	<4	26	1	8	0
Chocolate Graham & Marshmallow, Chewy Granola Bar, Quaker Oats, 1 bar (28 g)	120	<4	26	<2	11	0
Nut & Raisin, Chunky, Chewy Trail Mix Granola Bar, Quaker Oats, 1 bar (28 g)	120	5	38	1	8	0

FOOD/PORTION SIZE	CAL.	FAT Total (g)	FAT As % of Cal.	SAT. FAT Total (g)	SAT. FAT As % of Cal.	CHOL. (mg)
Oats n' Honey, Granola Bar, Nature Valley, 2 bars (47 g)	210	8	34	1	4	0
Peanut Butter Chocolate Chip, Chewy Granola Bar, Quaker Oats, 1 bar (28 g)	120	<5	34	<2	11	0
Variety Pack, Crunchy Granola Bar, Nature Valley, 2 bars (47 g)	210	8	34	1	1	0
POPCORN						
Air-popped, unsalted, 1 cup	30	tr	na	tr	na	0
Microwave, Butter, Light, Orville Redenbacher's, 2 tbsp. unpopped (32 g)	110	4	33	<1	4	0
Microwave, Original Butter, Pop Secret, 3 tbsp. unpopped (36 g)	170	12	64	3	16	0
Popped in vegetable oil, salted, 1 cup	55	3	49	<1	8	0
Sugar syrup coated, 1 cup	135	1	6	<1	<1	0
POTATO CHIPS						
FritoLays, about 18 chips (28 g)	150	10	60	<3	15	0
FritoLays, Hickory Bar-B-Que, about 15 chips (28 g)	150	10	60	2	12	0
Jay's, Crispy Ridged, about 15 chips, 1 oz. (28 g)	150	10	60	<2	9	0
Pringles, about 14 chips (28 g)	160	11	62	<3	14	0
Pringles Light, Ranch, about 16 crisps (28 g)	140	7	45	2	13	0
Pringles, Sour Cream n' Onion, about 14 crisps (28 g)	160	10	56	<3	14	0

SNACKS

FOOD/PORTION SIZE	CAL.	FAT Total (g)	FAT As % of Cal.	SAT. FAT Total (g)	SAT. FAT As % of Cal.	CHOL. (mg)
Ruffles, about 12 chips (28 g)	150	10	60	3	18	0
Ruffles, Choice, (40% less fat), about 16 chips, 1 oz. (28 g)	130	6	42	1	7	0

PRETZELS

Enriched flour, 2¼-in. sticks, 10 pretzels	10	tr	na	tr	na	0
Enriched flour, twisted, Dutch, 1 pretzel	65	1	14	<1	1	0
Enriched flour, twisted, thin, 10 pretzels	240	2	8	<1	1	0
Mister Salty, Sticks, 88 sticks (30 g)	110	1	8	0	0	0
Mister Salty, Twists, 9 pretzels (29 g)	110	<1	4	0	0	0
Pretzel Chips, Mr. Phipps, 16 chips, 1 oz. (28 g)	100	0	0	0	0	0
Rold Gold, Thin, Fat Free, about 10 pretzels (28 g)	110	0	0	0	0	0

Soups

FOOD/PORTION SIZE	CAL.	FAT Total (g)	FAT As % of Cal.	SAT. FAT Total (g)	SAT. FAT As % of Cal.	CHOL. (mg)
Asparagus, Cream of, Campbell's, 4 oz. condensed, 8 oz. as prepared 1 cup (120 mL)	110	7	57	2	16	5
Bean with bacon, canned, condensed, prepared with water, 1 cup	173	6	31	2	10	3
Beef broth bouillon consommé, canned, condensed, prepared with water, 1 cup	29	0	0	0	0	0

FOOD/PORTION SIZE	CAL.	FAT		SAT. FAT		CHOL. (mg)
		Total (g)	As % of Cal.	Total (g)	As % of Cal.	
Beef noodle, canned, condensed, prepared with water, 1 cup	85	3	32	1	11	5
Bouillon (chicken), *Wylers,* 1 cube	8	<1	na	0	0	0
Brocolli & Cheese, Lipton Cup of Soup, 1 envelope (16 g)	70	3	39	<2	19	<5
Chicken, cream of, canned, condensed, prepared with milk, 1 cup	190	11	52	5	24	27
Chicken, cream of, canned, condensed, prepared with water, 1 cup	115	7	55	2	16	10
Chicken noodle, canned, condensed, prepared with water, 1 cup	75	2	24	<1	8	7
Chicken noodle, dehydrated, prepared with water, 6 oz.	40	1	23	<1	5	3
Chicken Noodle, Hearty, Healthy Request, Campbell's, 1 cup (120 mL)	160	3	17	1	12	20
Chicken Noodle, Old Fashioned, Healthy Choice, 1 cup (250 g)	130	2	14	<1	3	10
Chicken Noodle, Progresso, 1 cup (238 g)	86	2	21	<1	5	20
Chicken rice, canned, condensed, prepared with water, 1 cup	60	2	30	<1	8	7
Clam chowder, New England, canned, condensed, prepared with milk, 1 cup	163	6	33	3	17	22
Minestrone, canned, condensed, prepared with water, 1 cup	80	3	34	<1	7	2

SOUPS

FOOD/PORTION SIZE	CAL.	FAT Total (g)	FAT As % of Cal.	SAT. FAT Total (g)	SAT. FAT As % of Cal.	CHOL. (mg)
Minestrone, Original Recipe, Progresso, 1 can (297 g)	160	4	23	<1	3	0
Mushroom, cream of, canned, condensed, prepared with milk, 1 cup	203	13	58	5	22	20
Mushroom, cream of, canned, condensed, prepared with water, 1 cup	129	9	63	3	21	2
Mushroom, Cream of, Healthy Request, Campbell's, condensed, ½ cup (120 mL)	70	3	39	1	13	10
Onion, dehydrated, prepared with water, 1 packet	20	tr	na	<1	5	0
Pea, green, canned, condensed, prepared with water, 1 cup	164	3	16	1	5	0
Tomato, canned, condensed, prepared with milk, 1 cup	160	6	34	3	17	17
Tomato, canned, condensed, prepared with water, 1 cup	85	2	21	<1	4	9
Tomato vegetable, dehydrated, prepared with water, 6 oz.	40	1	23	<1	7	0
Turkey Noodle, Campbell's, condensed, ½ cup (120 mL)	80	<3	28	1	11	15
Vegetable, Vegetarian, Campbell's, condensed, ½ cup (120 mL)	70	1	13	0	0	0
Vegetable beef, canned, condensed, prepared with water, 1 cup	80	2	23	<1	10	5

Vegetables

FOOD/PORTION SIZE	CAL.	FAT Total (g)	FAT As % of Cal.	SAT. FAT Total (g)	SAT. FAT As % of Cal.	CHOL. (mg)
ALFALFA						
Seeds, sprouted, raw, 1 cup	10	tr	na	tr	na	0
ARTICHOKES						
Globe or French, cooked, drained, 1 artichoke	53	tr	na	tr	na	0
Jerusalem, red, sliced, 1 cup	114	tr	na	0	0	0
ASPARAGUS						
Canned, spears, 4 spears	10	tr	na	tr	na	0
Cuts & tips, cooked, drained, from raw, 1 cup	45	1	20	<1	2	0
Cuts & tips, from frozen, 1 cup	50	1	18	<1	4	0
Spears, cooked, drained, from raw, 4 spears	15	tr	na	tr	na	0
Spears from frozen, 4 spears	15	tr	na	<1	6	0
BAMBOO SHOOTS						
Canned, drained, 1 cup	25	1	36	<1	4	0
BEANS						
Baby Lima, Birds Eye Regular Vegetables, approx. 3⅓ oz.	98	0	0	0	0	0
Fordhook Lima, Birds Eye Regular Vegetables, approx. 3⅓ oz.	94	0	0	0	0	0
Green, Cut, Birds Eye Regular Vegetables, 3 oz.	23	0	0	0	0	0
Green, French Cut, Birds Eye Deluxe, 3 oz.	25	0	0	0	0	0

VEGETABLES

FOOD/PORTION SIZE	CAL.	FAT Total (g)	FAT As % of Cal.	SAT. FAT Total (g)	SAT. FAT As % of Cal.	CHOL. (mg)
Green, Whole, Birds Eye Deluxe Vegetables, 3 oz.	25	0	0	0	0	0
Sprouts (mung), cooked, drained, 1 cup	25	tr	na	tr	na	0
BEETS						
Canned, drained, solids, diced or sliced, 1 cup	55	tr	na	tr	na	0
Cooked, drained, diced or sliced, 1 cup	55	tr	na	tr	na	0
Cooked, drained, whole, 2 beets	30	tr	na	tr	na	0
Greens, leaves and stems, cooked, drained, 1 cup	40	tr	na	tr	na	0
BROCCOLI						
Cooked, drained, from frozen, 1 piece (4½–5 in. long)	10	tr	na	tr	na	0
Cooked, drained, from frozen, chopped, 1 cup	50	tr	na	tr	na	0
Raw, 1 spear	40	1	23	<1	2	0
Spears from raw, cooked, drained, 1 cup (½-in. pieces)	45	tr	na	<1	2	0
BRUSSELS SPROUTS						
Cooked, drained, from frozen, 1 cup	65	1	14	<1	1	0
Cooked, drained, from raw, 1 cup	60	1	15	<1	3	0
CABBAGE						
Chinese pak-choi, cooked, drained, 1 cup	20	tr	na	tr	na	0
Chinese pe-tsai, raw, 1-in. pieces, 1 cup	10	tr	na	tr	na	0

FOOD/PORTION SIZE	CAL.	FAT Total (g)	FAT As % of Cal.	SAT. FAT Total (g)	SAT. FAT As % of Cal.	CHOL. (mg)
Common varieties, cooked, drained, 1 cup	30	tr	na	tr	na	0
Red, raw, coarsely shredded or sliced, 1 cup	20	tr	na	tr	na	0
Savoy, raw, coarsely shredded or sliced, 1 cup	20	tr	na	tr	na	0
CARROTS						
Canned, sliced, drained, solids, 1 cup	35	tr	na	<1	3	0
Cooked, sliced, drained, from frozen, 1 cup	55	tr	na	tr	na	0
Cooked, sliced, drained, from raw, 1 cup	70	tr	na	<1	1	0
Raw, w/o crowns or tips, scraped, grated, 1 cup	45	tr	na	tr	na	0
CAULIFLOWER						
Cooked, drained, from frozen (flowerets), 1 cup	35	tr	na	<1	3	0
Cooked, drained, from raw (flowerets), 1 cup	30	tr	na	tr	na	0
CELERY						
Pascal type, raw, large outer stalk, 1 stalk	5	tr	na	tr	na	0
Pascal type, raw, pieces, diced, 1 cup	20	tr	na	tr	na	0
COLLARDS						
Cooked, drained, from frozen (chopped), 1 cup	60	1	15	<1	2	0
Cooked, drained, from raw (leaves w/o stems), 1 cup	25	tr	na	<1	4	0

VEGETABLES

FOOD/PORTION SIZE	CAL.	FAT Total (g)	FAT As % of Cal.	SAT. FAT Total (g)	SAT. FAT As % of Cal.	CHOL. (mg)
CORN						
Sweet, canned, cream style, 1 cup	185	1	5	<1	1	0
Sweet, cooked, drained, from frozen, 1 ear (3½ in.)	60	tr	na	<1	2	0
Sweet, cooked, drained, from raw, 1 ear (5 x 1¾ in.)	85	1	11	<1	2	0
Sweet, cooked, drained, kernels, 1 cup	135	tr	na	tr	na	0
Sweet, vacuum packed, whole kernel, 1 cup	165	1	5	<1	1	0
CUCUMBER						
Peeled slices, ⅛-in. thick (large 2⅛-in. diameter, small 1¾-in. diameter), 6 large or 8 small	5	tr	na	tr	na	0
EGGPLANT						
Cooked, steamed, 1 cup	25	tr	na	tr	na	0
ENDIVE						
Curly (including escarole), raw, small pieces, 1 cup	10	tr	na	tr	na	0
GREENS						
Dandelion, cooked, drained, 1 cup	34	1	26	<1	3	0
Mustard, w/o stems and midribs, cooked, drained, 1 cup	20	tr	na	tr	na	0
Turnip, cooked, drained, from frozen (chopped), 1 cup	50	1	19	<1	4	0
Turnip, cooked, drained, from raw (leaves & stems), 1 cup	30	tr	na	<1	3	0

FOOD/PORTION SIZE	CAL.	FAT Total (g)	FAT As % of Cal.	SAT. FAT Total (g)	SAT. FAT As % of Cal.	CHOL. (mg)
KALE						
Cooked, drained, from frozen, chopped, 1 cup	40	1	23	<1	2	0
Cooked, drained, from raw, chopped, 1 cup	40	1	21	<1	2	0
KOHLRABI						
Thickened bulblike stem, cooked, drained, diced, 1 cup	50	tr	na	tr	na	0
LETTUCE						
Butterhead, as Boston types, raw, leaves, 1 outer leaf or 2 inner leaves	tr	tr	na	tr	na	0
Crisphead, as iceberg, raw, ¼ of head, 1 wedge	20	tr	na	tr	na	0
Crisphead, as iceberg, raw, pieces, chopped, shredded, 1 cup	5	tr	na	tr	na	0
Looseleaf (bunching varieties including romaine or cos), chopped or shredded, 1 cup	10	tr	na	tr	na	0
MIXED VEGETABLES						
Baby Carrots, Peas, Pearl Onions, Birds Eye Deluxe Vegetables, 3⅓ oz.	50	0	0	0	0	0
Bavarian Green Beans Spaetzle, Birds Eye International Recipe, 1 cup (151 g)	160	8	45	<5	25	50
Broccoli, Baby Carrots, Water Chestnuts, Birds Eye Farm Fresh Mix, ½ cup (95 g)	30	0	0	0	0	0

VEGETABLES

FOOD/PORTION SIZE	CAL.	FAT Total (g)	FAT As % of Cal.	SAT. FAT Total (g)	SAT. FAT As % of Cal.	CHOL. (mg)
Broccoli, Carrots & Water Chestnuts, Birds Eye Farm Fresh Mix, ½ cup	30	0	0	0	0	0
Broccoli, Cauliflower, Carrots, Birds Eye Farm Fresh Mix, ½ cup (92 g)	25	0	0	0	0	0
Broccoli, Red Pepper, Onion & Mushrooms, Birds Eye Farm Fresh Mix, ½ cup	25	0	0	0	0	0
Brussels Sprouts, Cauliflower, Carrots, Birds Eye Farm Fresh Mix, ½ cup (89 g)	30	0	0	0	0	0
Cauliflower in Cheese Sauce, Green Giant, ½ cup	60	<3	38	<1	8	<5
Green Beans, French, Toasted Almond, Birds Eye, ½ cup	70	<4	45	0	0	0
Green Peas, Pearl Onions, Green Giant, ½ cup	50	0	0	0	0	0
Italian Style, Birds Eye International Recipe, 3⅓ oz.	109	6	50	1	8	0
Japanese Style, Birds Eye International Recipe, ½ cup (127 g)	80	<5	51	3	34	10
Japanese Style, Birds Eye Stir-Fry Vegetables, prepared with soybean oil, 3⅓ oz.	120	8	60	1	8	0
New England Style Vegetables, Birds Eye International Recipe, 1 cup	190	11	52	4	19	15
Rice & Broccoli in Cheese Sauce, Green Giant, 1 container	320	12	34	4	11	15

FOOD/PORTION SIZE	CAL.	FAT Total (g)	FAT As % of Cal.	SAT. FAT Total (g)	SAT. FAT As % of Cal.	CHOL. (mg)
Spinach, Creamed, Green Giant, ½ cup	80	3	34	<2	17	0
Stir Fry Chinese Style, Birds Eye International Recipe, ½ cup (121 g)	45	0	0	0	0	0
MUSHROOMS						
Canned, drained, solids, 1 cup	35	tr	na	<1	3	0
Cooked, drained, 1 cup	40	1	23	<1	2	0
Raw, sliced or chopped, 1 cup	20	tr	na	tr	na	0
OKRA						
Pods, 3 x ⅝ in., cooked, 8 pods	27	tr	na	tr	na	0
ONIONS						
Cooked (whole or sliced), drained, 1 cup	60	tr	na	<1	2	0
Raw, chopped, 1 cup	55	tr	na	<1	2	0
Raw, sliced, 1 cup	40	tr	na	<1	2	0
Rings, breaded pan-fried, frozen, prepared, 2 rings	80	5	56	2	23	0
Spring, raw, bulb (⅜-in. diameter) and white portion of top, 6 onions	10	tr	na	tr	na	0
PARSLEY						
Freeze-dried, 1 tbsp.	tr	tr	tr	tr	tr	0
Raw, 10 sprigs	5	tr	na	tr	na	0
PARSNIPS						
Cooked, diced or 2-in. lengths, drained, 1 cup	125	tr	na	<1	<1	0

VEGETABLES

FOOD/PORTION SIZE	CAL.	FAT Total (g)	FAT As % of Cal.	SAT. FAT Total (g)	SAT. FAT As % of Cal.	CHOL. (mg)
PEAS						
Black-eyed, immature seeds, drained, from frozen, 1 cup	225	1	4	<1	1	0
Black-eyed, immature seeds, cooked, drained, from raw, 1 cup	180	1	5	<1	2	0
Green, canned, drained, solids, 1 cup	115	1	8	<1	1	0
Green, frozen, cooked, drained, 1 cup	125	tr	na	<1	1	0
Pods, edible, cooked, drained, 1 cup	65	tr	na	<1	1	0
PEPPERS						
Hot chili, raw, 1 pepper	20	tr	na	tr	na	0
Sweet (about 5 per lb., whole), stem and seeds removed, 1 pepper	20	tr	na	tr	na	0
Sweet (about 5 per lb., whole), stem and seeds removed, cooked, drained, 1 pepper	15	tr	na	tr	na	0
PICKLES						
Cucumber, dill, medium whole (3¾-in. long, 1¼-in. diameter), 1 pickle	5	tr	na	tr	na	0
Cucumber, fresh-pack slices, (1½-in. diameter, ¼-in. thick), 2 slices	10	tr	na	tr	na	0
Cucumber, sweet gherkin, small, (whole, about 2½-in. long, ¾-in. diameter), 1 pickle	20	tr	na	tr	na	0
Hamburger Dill Chips, Vlasic, 1 oz. (28 g)	5	0	0	0	0	0

FOOD/PORTION SIZE	CAL.	FAT Total (g)	FAT As % of Cal.	SAT. FAT Total (g)	SAT. FAT As % of Cal.	CHOL. (mg)
POTATOES						
Baked (about 2 per lb. raw), flesh only, 1 potato	145	tr	na	tr	na	0
Baked (about 2 per lb. raw), with skin, 1 potato	220	tr	na	<1	<1	0
Boiled (about 3 per lb. raw), peeled before boiling, 1 potato	115	tr	na	tr	na	0
French-Fried, Microwave Crinkle-Cut, Orelda, about 16 fries (84 g)	120	4	30	1	8	0
French fried strip (2 to 3½ in. long), fried in vegetable oil, 10 strips	160	8	45	3	17	0
French fried strip (2 to 3½ in. long), oven heated, 10 strips	110	4	33	2	16	0
Hot Tots, Orelda, 9 pieces (84 g)	150	7	42	<2	9	0
Red, raw, 1 potato, 5.5 oz. (148 g)	120	0	0	0	0	0
Sweet, candied, 2½ x 2-in. piece, 1 piece	145	3	19	1	6	8
Sweet, canned, solid packed, mashed, 1 cup	260	1	3	<1	<1	0
Sweet, cooked (baked in skin), 1 potato	115	tr	na	tr	na	0
Sweet, cooked (boiled w/o skin), 1 potato	160	tr	na	<1	<1	0
Sweet, vacuum pack, 2¾ x 1-in. piece	35	tr	na	tr	na	0
Twice-Baked, Orelda, 1 baker (140 g)	200	9	41	3	14	0
Wedges, Texas Crispers, Extra Spicy, Orelda, about 7 wedges (84 g)	170	10	53	<3	13	0

VEGETABLES

FOOD/PORTION SIZE	CAL.	FAT Total (g)	FAT As % of Cal.	SAT. FAT Total (g)	SAT. FAT As % of Cal.	CHOL. (mg)
PUMPKIN						
Canned, 1 cup	85	1	11	<1	4	0
Cooked, from raw, mashed, 1 cup	50	tr	na	<1	2	0
RADISHES						
Raw, stem ends and rootlets cut off, 4 radishes	5	tr	na	tr	na	0
SPINACH						
Cooked, drained, from frozen (leaf), 1 cup	55	tr	na	<1	2	0
Cooked, drained, from raw, 1 cup	40	tr	na	<1	2	0
Raw, chopped, 1 cup	10	tr	na	tr	na	0
SQUASH						
Summer (all varieties), cooked, sliced, drained, 1 cup	35	1	26	<1	3	0
TOMATOES						
Juice, canned, 1 cup	40	tr	na	tr	na	0
Paste, canned, 1 cup	220	2	8	<1	1	0
Puree, canned, 1 cup	105	tr	na	tr	na	0
Raw, 2³/₅-in. diameter (3 per 12-oz. pkg.), 1 tomato	25	tr	na	tr	na	0
Sauce, Canned, Contadina, ¼ cup (61 g)	20	0	0	0	0	0
Stewed, Canned, Contadina, ½ cup (124 g)	40	0	0	0	0	0

FOOD/PORTION SIZE	CAL.	FAT		SAT. FAT		CHOL. (mg)
		Total (g)	As % of Cal.	Total (g)	As % of Cal.	
VEGETABLES WITH SAUCE						
Broccoli with Cheese Sauce, Birds Eye Cheese Sauce Combination Vegetables, ½ cup (127 g)	70	3	39	<2	19	10
Brussels Sprouts in Butter Sauce, Green Giant, ⅔ cup (104 g)	60	<2	23	<1	8	<5
Cauliflower with Cheese Flavored Sauce, Green Giant, ½ cup (99 g)	60	<3	38	<1	8	<5
Italian Style Vegetables, Birds Eye International Recipe, 1 cup (159 g)	140	9	58	<4	23	15

Yogurt

FOOD/PORTION SIZE	CAL.	FAT		SAT. FAT		CHOL. (mg)
		Total (g)	As % of Cal.	Total (g)	As % of Cal.	
Blueberry, Dannon, 1 container (227 g)	240	3	11	<2	6	15
Blueberry, Dannon Light, 1 container (125 g)	50	0	0	0	0	0
Blueberry, Light 'n Lively, 1 container	140	1	6	<1	3	10
Cherry, Yoplait, 1 container (170 g)	170	<2	8	1	5	10
Peach, Perfectly, Frozen Yogurt, Edy's, ½ cup	100	<3	23	<2	14	10
Plain, Premium Lowfat, Dannon, 1 container (125 g)	140	4	26	2	13	20
Raspberry, Yoplait Fat Free, 1 container (170 g)	160	0	0	0	0	5

YOGURT

FOOD/PORTION SIZE	CAL.	FAT Total (g)	FAT As % of Cal.	SAT. FAT Total (g)	SAT. FAT As % of Cal.	CHOL. (mg)
Strawberry, Light, Nonfat, Dannon, 1 container (125 g)	50	0	0	0	0	0
Strawberry, Light, Yoplait, 6 oz. (170 g)	90	0	0	0	0	5
Strawberry, Yoplait, 1 container (170 g)	170	<2	8	1	5	10